JIHAD
WHAT EVERYONE NEEDS TO KNOW©

JIHAD

WHAT EVERYONE NEEDS TO KNOW©

ASMA AFSARUDDIN

OXFORD
UNIVERSITY PRESS

OXFORD
UNIVERSITY PRESS

Oxford University Press is a department of the University of Oxford. It furthers
the University's objective of excellence in research, scholarship, and education
by publishing worldwide. Oxford is a registered trade mark of Oxford University
Press in the UK and certain other countries.

"What Everyone Needs to Know" is a registered trademark of
Oxford University Press.

Published in the United States of America by Oxford University Press
198 Madison Avenue, New York, NY 10016, United States of America.

Library of Congress Control Number: 2021920937
ISBN 978–0–19–064732–2 (pbk.)
ISBN 978–0–19–064731–5 (hbk.)

DOI: 10.1093/oso/9780190647315.001.0001

1 3 5 7 9 8 6 4 2

Paperback printed by LSC Communications, United States of America
Hardback printed by Bridgeport National Bindery, Inc., United States of America

CONTENTS

ACKNOWLEDGMENTS   XI

Introduction   **1**

1 Jihad in the Quran and Commentary Literature   **9**

What is the basic meaning of jihad?   10

How often does the word "jihad" occur in the Quran?   11

Does the Quran refer to different forms of jihad?   11

Does the Quran refer to the spiritual jihad?   12

What does jihad mean in the Meccan period?   13

Did jihad have a military meaning in the Meccan period?   16

What does jihad mean in the Medinan period?   17

Is only defensive fighting allowed in the Quran?   19

Is jihad in the Quran holy war?   23

*Can Muslims continue to fight when the enemy stops fighting and
seeks peace?*   24

Are the peaceful verses in the Quran abrogated by the "sword verse?" 26

Are Christians and Jews singled out for fighting in the Quran?   29

Does the Quran tell Muslims not to be friends with Jews and Christians? 33

Does the Quran support offensive military activity to spread Islam? 34

Is the military jihad a permanent religious obligation in the Quran?   37

What motivated the military conquests that took place after the
death of Muhammad?   39

What does the Quran say about martyrdom?   41

Is the religious status of a military martyr higher than that of other
Muslims?   42

Is suicide permitted in the Quran?   44

Is terrorism condoned in the Quran?   44

2 Jihad in the Hadith Literature   47

What does "jihad" mean in the hadith literature?   49

Do hadiths describe how a military jihad should be carried out?   54

How should we understand the hadith that commands Muslims to
fight non-Muslims until they accept Islam?   55

What does the hadith literature say about martyrdom?   56

How can one know for sure that someone has attained martyrdom?   59

Are there certain hadiths that appear to contradict the Quran on
martyrdom?   60

Is there a hadith that promises the reward of seventy-two virgins to
battlefield martyrs?   61

Does the hadith literature encourage seeking martyrdom?   63

Are there distinctly Shii views on martyrdom?   64

What does the hadith literature say about suicide and terrorism?   65

What are the greater and lesser jihads?   65

Do standard collections list hadiths that describe nonmilitary aspects
of jihad?   66

3 Jihad in the Legal Literature   70

How did Muslim jurists understand jihad?   71

How is war declared and by whom according to jurists?   73

Can civilians ever be targeted during a military attack?   74

How did jurists view martyrdom?   76

How are prisoners of war to be treated?   77

Can Muslims fight under corrupt rulers?   79

Did jurists allow offensive military jihad?   80

Did jurists consider the military jihad to be holy war?   83

Can women take part in the military jihad?   85

Can Jews, Christians, and other non-Muslims take part
in the military jihad?   87

Why did the medieval jurists divide the world into the Abode of Islam
and Abode of War?   88

Does the division of the world into the Abode of Islam and Abode of
War still apply in the modern period?   90

Did jurists permit suicide attacks?   91

What are the views of jurists on terrorism?   92

**4 Jihad in Morally Edifying, Ethical, and Mystical
    Literature   94**

What does jihad mean in the daily life of the average believer?   95

Is the military jihad deemed to be the highest form of human struggle?   98

What is the greater struggle?   100

Why do some people resist the idea that the spiritual jihad is a
genuine part of jihad?   100

Is the spiritual struggle carried out mainly by mystics?   103

Are there references to nonmilitary forms of jihad in early Islamic
writings?   103

How do Muslim mystics practice the internal, greater jihad?   105

Did jurists refer to the spiritual jihad in their writings?   108

**5 Jihad as Conceived by Modern Political
    Revolutionaries and Militants   111**

How do modern militants in the Islamic world understand jihad?   113

Which early thinkers influenced modern political revolutionaries and
militants?   113

Who are other influential sources for modern militant groups?   115

What is the Jahiliyya?   118

How do militant Islamists justify their violent attacks on other
Muslims and non-Muslims?   119

Have Shii thinkers called for political revolution as a form of jihad in
the twentieth century?   122

What were Usama bin Laden's views on jihad?   124

What are "martyrdom operations" and when did they start?   126

How do militant Islamists justify suicide attacks?   126

How does ISIS justify its violent actions as jihad?   129

Where are the "moderate" Muslims and why do they not denounce
extremism?   130

6 Jihad in the Thought of Modern and Contemporary Mainstream Scholars   132

How do modern Muslim scholars understand the military jihad?   133

What do modern Muslim scholars say about abrogation in the Quran?   133

Are there Muslim scholars who have challenged the views of
Islamist militants?   136

Are there Muslim scholars who have denounced the views of Usama
bin Laden and his followers after the September 11 attacks?   141

Are there Muslim scholars speaking out against suicide bombings?   143

Why don't Muslim scholars collectively denounce terrorism?   145

Have Muslim scholars denounced ISIS and its militant views?   146

What are the main differences between militants and mainstream
scholars of Islam today on the issue of violence?   146

7 Jihad as Nonviolent Struggle and Peacemaking   148

Is there pacifism in Islam?   149

Can jihad be understood as nonviolent struggle and peacemaking?   150

Which Muslim thinkers understand jihad as nonviolent struggle?   151

*What caused the modern turn toward thinking of jihad as nonviolent
struggle?*   153

Is there a theological basis in Islam for promoting peace?   155

Do Muslim peace activists reject the military jihad?   158

8 Jihad and Its Perceptions in the West   162

Is there a Western equivalent of the military jihad?   164

*Is there an Islamic influence on the development of modern
international law?*   165

*Is classical Islamic international law compatible with modern
international law?*   166

*Are there modern Muslim critics of the concepts of the Abodes of
War and Peace?*   168

How does the Western media portray jihad?   170

*Does the American media cover violent acts carried out by Muslims
differently than those carried out by non-Muslims?*   172

How does Hollywood portray jihad and Muslims?   174

How does the internet affect public perceptions of jihad in the West? 175

*Are there Western militants who are influenced by Islamophobic
rhetoric on jihad?*   176

*How can one challenge anti-Islamic discourses that distort the
meanings of jihad?*   180

*Can educational institutions play a role in providing balanced
information about jihad?*   182

GLOSSARY: IMPORTANT NAMES, PLACES, EVENTS, AND TERMS   185
BIBLIOGRAPHY   195
INDEX   199

ACKNOWLEDGMENTS

This book is intended for a broad readership. Its style is meant to be accessible, without being weighed down by the usual scholarly apparatus of dense and copious footnotes. I have also dispensed with the painstaking transliteration of Arabic names and terms and have adopted simplified spellings that will be more appealing to the nonspecialist English reader. It should be noted that when I introduce a new Arabic term, it is italicized at its first occurrence in each chapter and then subsequently written without italics. Many of these Arabic terms and names are repeated in the glossary at the end of the book. All dates are Common Era (Gregorian) and indicated by CE. For those who may lament the lack of footnotes in this book, I am happy to direct their attention to my longer (and densely footnoted!) book titled *Striving in the Path of God: Jihad and Martyrdom in Islamic Thought* (Oxford University Press, 2013), which provides full documentation for many of the points made in this work. Readers are encouraged to consult this earlier book as well as other publications listed in the bibliography.

An endeavor of this kind can only benefit from the input of colleagues and friends. I would like to take this opportunity to express my gratitude to John Voll of Georgetown University who took the time out of his very busy schedule to read the full draft of the book. His astute observations and comments were very insightful. Thanks are furthermore due to Mohammad Fadel of the University of Toronto and Tom Heneghan, former religion editor for Reuters and currently a freelance journalist, both of whom read parts of the manuscript and weighed in with their helpful feedback. I also acknowledge the helpful clarifications provided by Timothy Waters of Indiana University on points of modern international law. And, of course, I am grateful to Cynthia Read, indefatigable Executive Editor at Oxford University Press, who invited me to write this volume for the well-known *What Everybody Needs To Know* series and provided valuable guidance and feedback every step of the way. Her editorial assistant Brent Matheny was a model of efficiency and kept things moving at a brisk pace.

I also need to recognize various family members who kept me honest by constantly inquiring about the progress of this book and encouraging me to race towards the finish line. They include my mother, Maleka Khatun, sister Najma Hasib, and brother-in-law, Mansur Hasib. And, finally, I have to acknowledge the special debt I owe my husband, Steve Vinson, for the moral support he always provides. He also read the whole manuscript and was generous with incisive comments and suggestions for improvement from which I benefitted greatly. Needless to say, remaining shortcomings are mine alone.

Asma Afsaruddin
Bloomington, Indiana
September 13, 2021

INTRODUCTION

The word *jihad* seems to be everywhere. It is frequently used, especially in the Western media, to refer to violent acts carried out by militants from Muslim backgrounds as part of a civilizational battle against the West. This is what even an educated non-Muslim in the West tends to reflexively associate with jihad; this perspective overwhelmingly colors public rhetoric about Islam and Muslims today. This is, however, a highly distorted understanding of a concept whose basic meaning is "struggle," "striving," "utmost effort." For most Muslims, jihad represents the highest human struggle to promote and carry out what is morally good, just, and noble in all walks of life and to prevent what is morally wrong, unjust, and degrading to humans and all creatures. Such a struggle can and should be carried out by a variety of means, depending on the context: moral, ethical, spiritual, mental, intellectual, verbal, financial, physical, and military.

Jihad is, therefore, a *polyvalent* term; that is to say, it is a word that contains within it layers of meaning that become apparent in specific circumstances. This is why the concept of jihad needs to be considered from multiple perspectives: scriptural, theological, moral, ethical, legal, and sociopolitical. This book is intended to cover these multiple aspects of jihad. When I use the word "jihad" in general, I am broadly referring to the struggle of human beings to live their lives on earth in decent and morally praiseworthy ways and realize their full potential as human beings. Muslims understand this ongoing human struggle to be in accordance with the will of God. When I refer to the martial aspects of jihad, I use the term "military jihad" or "combative jihad" to indicate that it is being used in this limited sense. Observations about the military or combative jihad and rules governing it do not apply to other aspects of human striving on earth in specific sociocultural, spiritual, and intellectual realms.

The book emphasizes what I describe as a "holistic" approach to the complex concept of jihad. It adopts an approach that considers the term's various dimensions without unduly privileging the legal and military aspects of this term, as is usually the case. This work aims to provide a guide to the diverse understandings of jihad through time, from the early centuries of Islam until the contemporary period. By collecting this information in a single source, it is hoped the book will be a helpful resource for all those interested in an accessible treatment of this topic, grounded in scholarly sources: undergraduate and graduate students; specialists and nonspecialists, academics, public intellectuals, policymakers, journalists, and a general educated readership.

The book addresses key questions and (mis)perceptions about jihad that are common today in the West (and beyond). These popular (mis)perceptions are often based on three main assumptions:

1. Jihad is relentless, bloody warfare to be waged by all Muslims against all non-Muslims until Islam occupies the whole world or till the end of time—whichever occurs first.
2. Muslims can issue the call for such a jihad anytime and anywhere, with the sole excuse that stubborn unbelievers will not politically submit, willingly or unwillingly, at their hands. Militant groups today who declare "jihad" on their own against non-Muslims *and* against Muslims with whom they disagree are thus following a basic duty within Islam.

3. Muslims who argue that a true military jihad is primarily defensive and conditional while the internal, nonviolent jihad is continuous and unconditional are deliberately lying about the real nature of jihad and should be regarded as apologists for their faith.

It is not only anti-Islamic (Islamophobic) websites that present such perceptions of jihad. Popular media outlets and many mainstream publications produced in the West frequently convey approximate versions of this and contribute to the formation of such views. Militant Islamist websites and print literature often reinforce such ideas. In support of militant views, these latter sources provide selective quotations from the Quran, hadith, and legal literature without any reference to their historical contexts or their contested interpretations. To the average consumer of such sources, these views may seem quite compelling indeed.

When relevant, I provide a brief overview of the current debates concerning jihad in the global public sphere, as well as in the more cloistered space of academia. Toward the end of the book there is discussion of how politicized and ideological these public conversations have become, first in the aftermath of September 11 and, more recently, after the 2016 US presidential elections that brought Donald Trump to power. In the wake of these developments, this book provides a historically grounded treatment of this topic in an accessible question-and-answer format.

In Chapter 1, titled "Jihad in the Quran and Commentary Literature," I discuss the basic meanings of the term "jihad" and its main components in the Quran, Islam's central scripture. Key Quranic verses are highlighted and a brief survey of the relevant views of both premodern and modern Quran commentators (exegetes) on these verses is provided.

There is also a focus on the contextualization of such views in their appropriate sociohistorical circumstances so that the reader can appreciate how different exegetes from different

time periods tended to understand key Quranic verses in specific ways. This chapter also addresses the knotty question of
the concept of "abrogation" (in Arabic *naskh*). According to
this concept adopted by a number of Muslim scholars, certain
early passages of the Quran may be considered to have been
superseded, if not actually abrogated or cancelled, by later
revelations. This position is much debated within the Islamic
commentary tradition as well as in legal circles. Therefore, one
of the questions I take up in that chapter is whether peaceful
verses in the Quran can be considered to be abrogated, as some
maintain, by later belligerent verses revealed in different historical circumstances.

Another much-debated question I address is the concept of
the internal or spiritual jihad, and whether it is endorsed in
the Quran or if it represents a later construction by "marginal"
mystical groups. A final critical question is whether suicide (the
deliberate taking of one's life) and terrorism are permissible
according to the Quran, since the adoption of suicide bombing
by militants in a number of Muslim-majority societies is often
assumed to be based on Islamic doctrine.

Chapter 2 discusses jihad as represented in the hadith literature. Hadith refers to sayings attributed to the Prophet
Muhammad (d. 632). Those sayings determined to be sound
and reliable are considered normative or binding for Muslims.
Most hadith works typically contain a section on jihad. A comparison of the content of these jihad sections in early and
later hadith works can provide valuable evidence for gradual
changes in the conceptualizations of jihad. A key question is
the identification of those hadiths on jihad that are generally
considered reliable and those that are not.

Jihad as represented in the legal literature is the focus of
Chapter 3. Jurists, in contrast to Quran commentators, hadith
scholars, and moral theologians, mainly dealt with jihad as
a military obligation of the state to ensure the security of its
inhabitants against external threats. It is in these legal works
composed after the second century of Islam (corresponding to

the eighth century CE) where we start to see a fuller articulation of the laws of war and peace. These works often drew
upon Quranic verses and the *sunna* (the normative practices)
of the Prophet in crafting specific rules that governed carrying
out armed combat. But some controversial legal positions
had no relation to these two sources but were rather based
on Realpolitik—they took shape as hard-headed, practical
responses to the political and historical circumstances of
the time.

Some of these controversial legal positions feed widespread
assumptions about the nature and purpose of the military
jihad. Privileging the legal literature above other kinds of literature in discussions of jihad almost inevitably leads to the conclusion that it is primarily a military obligation imposed upon
able-bodied Muslim men in the service of state and religion.

Accordingly, one of the main questions I deal with in
Chapter 3 has to do with the particular concerns and priorities
of jurists that led them to view the military jihad through a
certain lens in differing sociopolitical circumstances. An important historical question is whether the premodern division
of the world by certain jurists into the Abode/House of Islam
(*Dar al-Islam*) and Abode/House of War (*Dar al-Harb*) still
holds in the modern period. I also consider whether specific
premodern legal pronouncements on carrying out military
jihad that reflected a different world order are still valid in the
contemporary period.

My holistic approach to the topic of jihad allows me to more
comprehensively reconstruct the meanings contained within
the term "jihad" and the longer phrase *al-jihad fi sabil allah*
(striving in the path of God). This is what I do in Chapter 4,
titled "Jihad in Morally Edifying and Theological Literature."
In that chapter, I survey a broader range of literary sources.
Writings focused on moral, ethical, and spiritual issues composed by scholars of various stripes emphasize *sabr* (patient
forbearance) as the main component of jihad in the realms of
religious ethics and public conduct.

The concerns of moral theologians and ethicists were markedly different from those of jurists, which affected how they prioritized the meanings of jihad. In this context, I explore the moral and ethical implications of jihad in the daily life of the average believer and not just in legal and administrative circles.

The chapter affords me the opportunity to connect the dots between the Quranic concept of sabr and what in the later literature becomes labeled as the "spiritual struggle" par excellence (*jihad al-nafs*). This is a connection that has generally been overlooked or ignored in works produced by Western academics studying Islam and the Middle East. I show instead that the internal spiritual and moral dimensions of jihad are essential ingredients of mainstream Muslim devotional practices and rooted in the foundational texts of Islam.

In Chapter 5, I discuss how jihad is portrayed in modern and contemporary militant literature. Militant literature portrays jihad as a cosmic (universal) battle until the end of time. The ultimately victorious group will consist of "right-thinking" Muslims who constitute the camp favored by God: That is to say, mainly themselves to the exclusion of other Muslims who do not think like them. An examination of sociohistorical and political factors helps explain the rise of militancy and the co-optation of religious symbols and concepts, particularly jihad, to this end.

I also examine the ways these militants' views differ from those of classical scholars and trace these differences to specific historical and political factors. A very important question to be addressed is the grisly phenomenon of suicide bombing: On what basis do militants justify suicide bombing as a part of legitimate jihad? I discover—surprisingly—a range of views among them.

Chapter 6 is titled "Jihad in the Thought of Modern and Contemporary Mainstream Scholars" and draws attention to the voices of mainstream Muslim scholars and public intellectuals who provide compelling refutations of militant positions. These scholars and thinkers deal with the concept of jihad in a contextualized and holistic manner and emphasize its historically conditioned multiple meanings through time. Typically they acknowledge that armed combat has been and must continue to be a necessary feature of jihad under specific circumstances—but that it is by no means the only significant aspect of this complex term. These thinkers engage the Islamic tradition in all its diversity, as it developed from the seventh century up to the present time. They emphasize the multiple discourses that have grown up around jihad in response to the demands of specific sociopolitical circumstances.

Chapter 7 focuses on jihad as a peacemaking enterprise. A number of modern and contemporary scholars and activists have focused in their written works on the peaceful activism they understand to be the predominant meaning of jihad. Such individuals typically emphasize the virtue of patient forbearance (sabr) as the most important aspect of jihad, and, therefore, of nonviolent resistance to wrongdoing. This emphasis on nonviolent activism as the best expression of jihad is very much a modern phenomenon that nevertheless appeals to the Quran, hadith, and historical practices of early Muslims for legitimation.

Chapter 8 discusses how jihad tends to be viewed and imagined in the West (primarily in the United States and Western Europe). Almost without exception, jihad is described in Western media outlets, the internet, and even in academic circles as "holy war." From this perspective, the roots of militant Islamism are understood to be grounded in Islam's foundational texts. Furthermore, through this lens, violent military activity is portrayed as a fundamental religious obligation for Muslims. The chapter explores how and why these perceptions are so deeply rooted in the West and how they tend to promote Islamophobia (fear of Islam).

The chapter also points to similarities between the military jihad and the Christian concept of "just war." It probes the probable influence of the Islamic law of nations on the development of modern international law, particularly in connection with the principle of "just conduct" during legitimate warfare, a concept that developed very late in the Western just war tradition.

And now on to a discussion of the polyvalent term "jihad" in the Quran—for without an understanding of the Quranic jihad, we cannot understand the concept's richness and complexities, the human interpretations of which have had and continue to have a lasting effect on our contemporary world.

1

JIHAD IN THE QURAN AND COMMENTARY LITERATURE

The term "jihad" and words related to it occur several times in the Quran. The Quran (which means "Recitation" and "Reading" in Arabic) is a text divinely revealed to the Prophet Muhammad, as Muslims believe. The revelations started roughly in the year 610 CE in Mecca and continued for approximately twenty-two years until the Prophet's death in Medina in 632 CE. Both Mecca and Medina are cities in what is now Saudi Arabia.

Each chapter of the Quran is typically assigned to either the Meccan or Medinan periods of the Prophet's life. Chapters belonging to the Meccan period refer to the revelations that came to Muhammad while he lived in Mecca (between roughly 610 and 622). Medinan chapters date from the time when the Prophet emigrated to Medina from Mecca in 622; this event, known in Arabic as the *hijra* (emigration, migration), also marks the beginning of the Islamic calendar. The Medinan period ends with Muhammad's death ten years later and refers to the years between 622 and 632.

Muslim scholars sometimes disagreed among themselves about the precise dating of individual Quranic verses. There is, however, broad agreement concerning the general attribution of the chapters to the Meccan or Medinan periods based on their connection to specific events in Muhammad's life and on shared thematic and stylistic features. The Quranic text itself is not arranged according to chronological order but according to the length of the chapters, proceeding from the longest to the shortest. (The first short chapter, consisting of seven verses, is the exception).

The Quran is not only a written text meant to be silently read and reflected upon but is also a liturgical text that is memorized and recited orally during worship. During the month of Ramadan when Muslims fast from daybreak to sunset, the entire text of the Quran is commonly recited in mosques during special congregational prayers held at night. It is also recited during many of life's significant occasions, such as the birth of a child, marriage, and death. The Quran is always recited in Arabic. This reflects the Muslim's belief that the entire Quran is a transcript of God's revelations to Muhammad; its message cannot be fully appreciated and understood except in its original language of revelation. Translations into other languages are plentiful but do not substitute for the original Arabic text. According to Islamic doctrine, God (called Allah in Arabic, a divine name also used by Arabic-speaking Christians and Jews) is the author of the Quran. This divine authorship invests its sacred text with a majesty and authoritativeness that no other text of human origin can approach.

Given the centrality of the Quran to everything Islamic, we must start our discussion by focusing on how the term "jihad" and related terms are used in various passages of the Quran. This will help us understand the original scripture-based meanings and functions of these terms. Quranic verses cited are bolded in the text to make it easier to pick them out. Translations are generally mine, although I have consulted published translations.

What is the basic meaning of jihad?

The basic meaning of jihad is "struggle," "striving," "exertion." The word "jihad" is derived from the Arabic root *j-h-d*. In Arabic, words typically have three consonants in their roots. These root consonants combine with vowels and certain prefixes and infixes (additional internal letters) to generate different verbal forms and a range of related meanings.

Jihad is a verbal noun from the third verbal form in Arabic, which generally implies an action extended to another person or object. The verb behind jihad is *jāhada*. The long vowel *a* in Arabic is romanized here as *ā*; this is a feature of the third verbal form. (Diacritics or special characters, like the macron, or dash above letters, will be used very sparingly in this book.) The verb *jāhada*, according to the early Arabic-language scholars, means "to strive, labor, or toil; to exert oneself or one's power or efforts or endeavors or ability." Jihad as the verbal noun, therefore, conveys these basic meanings of striving, exertion, effort.

How often does the word "jihad" occur in the Quran?

Forty-one verses containing words derived from the root *j-h-d*, mostly as verbal forms, occur in the Quranic text. The noun jihad itself (in this exact form) occurs only four times in the Quran. The longer Arabic phrase *al-jihad fi sabil allah* (meaning "striving in the path of God") does not occur in the Quran in this exact phrasing but is common in extra-Quranic literature. Instead, the Quran uses verbal forms derived from *j-h-d*, often in the form of commands, with the phrase *fi sabil allah* (in the path of/for the sake of God). For example, it commands in Arabic: *wa-jāhidū bi-amwalikum wa-anfusikum fi sabil allah* (Quran 9:41). This translates as **"And strive with your wealth and your selves in the path of God."**

Harb, the Arabic word for "war" in general, is never used in the Quran with the phrase "in the path of God" and is not related to the concept of jihad.

Does the Quran refer to different forms of jihad?

Yes it does. Jihad in the Quran is a broad concept and refers in general to the human struggle on earth to live and flourish through worship of God and the realization of his will. This struggle includes making the effort to cultivate and promote what is right and good and prevent what is wrong and harmful in all spheres of life through a variety of means. The duty to undertake this moral and ethical struggle is clearly established in the Quran (Quran 3:104, 3:110, 9:71, 9:112, 22:41, and others).

Two main aspects of jihad become apparent in the Quran during the Meccan and Medinan periods. The first aspect—known in Arabic as *sabr*—is prominent in the Meccan chapters and retains its importance in the Medinan chapters as well. The second aspect—known in Arabic as *qital*—makes its appearance in the Medinan period and is a conditional aspect of jihad.

Sabr can be translated into English in several ways: patience, forbearance, steadfastness, perseverance, and a kind of stoicism, among other possibilities. For the most part, I have adopted the translation "patient forbearance"; in some instances, other translations will be used in this book depending on the context. Sabr, or patient forbearance, is the constant feature of jihad throughout the Quran, since no worthwhile human endeavor can be carried out without exercising this trait.

Qital refers specifically to fighting when just cause and intention are present. The conditions during which fighting is allowed are clearly outlined in the Quran.

Does the Quran refer to the spiritual jihad?

It does indeed. The Quranic term "sabr" in fact refers to the internal and spiritual jihad that must be continuously carried out to fulfill one's obligations to God and one's fellow beings. This internal struggle indicated by sabr is the earliest aspect of jihad and an essential part of it. Those who maintain the position that there is no spiritual, noncombative dimension to jihad in the Quran have failed to recognize the importance of sabr, or patient forbearance, and its organic connection to jihad within the Quranic text.

One very important Quranic verse (3:200) highlights the importance of cultivating and practicing patient forbearance in one's life. It states: **"O those who believe, be patient and forbearing, outdo others in forbearance, be firm, and revere God so that you may succeed."**

The early Muslim scholar Abu Salama ibn Abd al-Rahman (d. ca. 722) said that this verse commands Muslims "to be vigilant concerning the performance of the prayers, one after the other." Muslims, as is well-known, pray five times a day. Frequent daily prayers are acts that require considerable patience and effort on the part of the worshipper. Many Quran commentators, like the famous exegete Muhammad ibn Jarir al-Tabari (d. 923), commented that the general understanding of this verse is that it advises believers to be steadfast in their religion and in obedience to God. The command contained in Quran 3:200 includes "all the various forms of obedience to God regarding what He has commanded and what He has prohibited, the difficult and the exacting, the easy and the simple," says al-Tabari. In other words, the verse emphasizes that patient forbearance is a trait that should be practiced in all spheres of life by the faithful as they struggle to obey God and carry out their religious duties.

The Quran promises generous rewards in the hereafter to the righteous who practice patient forbearance in this world. One verse, Quran 39:10, states that **"those who are patient will be given their reward without measure."** Another verse, Quran 25:75, states **"They will be awarded the heavenly chamber for what they bore in patience and will be met there with greetings and [words of] peace."**

What does jihad mean in the Meccan period?

Verbs derived from the Arabic root *j-h-d* are used several times in Meccan verses. These verses urge the early Muslims to strive to fulfill God's commands in their lives and to preach the faith publicly. Three of these verses are worthy of discussion: Quran 29:69; 25:52; and 22:78.

Quran 29:69 states: **"As for those who struggle in regard to us [*jāhadū fina*], we will surely guide them to our paths."** The eighth-century exegete (Quran commentator) Muqatil ibn Sulayman (d. 767) explains this verse as referring to those who do good deeds for the sake of God and is similar to Quran 22:78. **"We will guide them to our paths"** means that they will be guided to Islam and that God provides help for those who do good, he says. The tenth-century exegete Ibn Atiyya (d. 993) commented that because this verse was revealed in the Medinan period before fighting was allowed, jihad in this verse must be understood to refer to a general striving to fulfill one's religious obligations and to seek God's satisfaction.

Exegetes in subsequent centuries tend to repeat these views. In the late twelfth century, the highly esteemed Quran commentator Fakhr al-Din al-Razi (d. 1210) emphasized that this verse urges Muslims to obey God to the best of one's ability and to attempt to understand the truth by critically examining the divine proofs contained in the Quran. For al-Razi, jihad in this verse refers to both a spiritual and intellectual effort.

Quran 25:52 states **"Do not obey the unbelievers and strive *with it* against them mightily [*jihad kabir*]."** There is an overwhelming consensus among commentators that in this verse Muhammad is being divinely directed to strive against falsehood with the truths contained in the Quran—that is, by verbally proclaiming the divine message being communicated to him. The pronoun "it" used in the verse is a reference to the Quran. This kind of striving is deemed by Muslim scholars to constitute "jihad of the tongue." These struggles on the part of the Prophet to communicate the word of God are described as "a great effort" (*jihad kabir*) on account of the great hardships he faced while carrying out this command.

Quran 22:78, states: **"Strive in regard to God a true striving as is His due."** This verse is usually dated between the late Meccan period and the early Medinan period, when Muslims had not yet been granted permission to militarily defend themselves. In the eighth century, the Quran commentator, Muqatil ibn Sulayman, understands this verse to require humans to "do good deeds for God as is His due." He notes that the Arabic command in this verse *jāhidū* (related to the noun jihad and meaning "strive!" addressed to a collectivity of people) urges humans to excel in the performance of good deeds to earn divine approval. Another early scholar Ibn al-Mubarak (d. 797) is said to have understood this verse as referring to "striving against one's desires and the lower self."

These three verses clearly show that jihad (and related words) in the Meccan period have the general meaning of striving to please God through worship and the carrying out of good deeds to the best of one's abilities. However, some later scholars understood Quran 22:78 to refer additionally to striving through armed combat. Thus the well-known twelfth-century exegete al-Zamakhshari (d. 1144) understood the verse as referring to both striving against one's base desires and striving against the enemy through military means.

There are other Meccan verses that encourage the faithful to strive actively to do good and prevent wrongdoing while practicing patient forbearance. One such verse (16:110) states: **"As for those who after persecution emigrated and strove actively [*jāhadū*] and were patient [*sabaru*] to the last, your Lord will be forgiving and merciful to them on the day when every soul will come pleading for itself."** Since this is a Meccan verse, some commentators suggest that the reference to emigration should be understood as a reference to the emigration to Abyssinia (current-day Ethiopia) by an early group of Muslims roughly around 613–614, about a decade before the historically more significant emigration to Medina took place in 622.

Another Meccan verse (Quran 29:6) states: **"The one who strives [*jāhada*] strives for oneself; for God has no need of**

anything in all his creation." These instances of jihad, or striving, in the Meccan period do not have anything to do with military activity; rather, they are references to the term's basic meaning of personally struggling to do what is good and morally excellent as part of one's earthly existence.

Did jihad have a military meaning in the Meccan period?

During the Meccan period, the Muslims were not given divine permission to physically retaliate against the pagan Meccans, who were severely persecuting them for their monotheistic faith. According to the commentary and biographical literature on Muhammad, the pagan Meccans instituted harsh measures against the Muslims—including an economic boycott, forced starvation, and physical torture—to make them give up their new faith and return to the idol worship of their forefathers. Verses revealed during the Meccan period advise Muslims to steadfastly endure the hostility of the Meccans while continuing to profess their monotheistic beliefs and practice their faith. Although the Quran recognizes the right to self-defense for those who are wronged, it maintains in this early period that to bear patiently the wrongdoing of others and to forgive those who cause them harm is the superior course of action. A cluster of verses (42:40–43) reveal this highly significant, non-militant dimension of struggling against wrongdoing (and, therefore, of jihad) in this early phase of Muhammad's prophetic career. These verses state:

> **The recompense of evil is evil similar to it: but, whoever pardons and makes peace, his reward rests with God—for indeed, He does not love evil-doers.**
> **As for those who defend themselves after having been wronged—there is no recourse against them: recourse is against those who oppress people and behave unjustly on earth, offending against all right; for them**

awaits grievous suffering. But if one is patient in adversity and forgives, then that is indeed the best way to resolve matters.

These verses emphasize the importance of practicing patient forbearance and forgiving those who cause one harm as part of the continuous jihad to promote what is right and prevent what is wrong through moral and ethical means. Military activity does not figure in these verses.

What does jihad mean in the Medinan period?

Nonviolent struggle against injustice and persecution, as well as patient forbearance in the face of harm, continued to be endorsed in the Medinan period. One Medinan verse (47:31) states: "**We shall indeed test you so that we may know the active strivers [*al-mujahidin*] and the quietly forbearing [*al-sabirin*] among you, and we will test your affairs.**" Here the term "mujahidin" (those who strive actively) should be understood in the broadest sense; the context does not imply any kind of military action. The active strivers complement those who are quietly forbearing—both resort to praiseworthy ways of dealing with life's trials and the harm others cause. It should be noted here that nonviolent struggle is not the same as passivity, which when displayed in the face of grave oppression and injustice, is clearly marked as immoral in the Quran. "Those who are passive" earn divine rebuke in Quran 4:95.

Roughly two years after Muhammad's emigration to Medina in 622, a new feature of jihad appeared—that of defensive fighting signified by the Arabic term "qital." The Quran provides a number of reasons for resorting to armed combat against a hostile enemy that has already carried out aggression against Muslims. Quran 22:39–40 are believed by the majority of scholars to have been the first verses revealed to

Muhammad allowing fighting, which led to the Battle of Badr in 624. These verses state:

> **Permission is given to those against whom fighting has been initiated because they have been wronged, and God is able to help them. These are they who have been wrongfully expelled from their homes merely for saying "God is our Lord." If God had not restrained some people by means of others, monasteries, churches, synagogues, and mosques in which God's name is mentioned frequently would have been destroyed. Indeed God comes to the aid of those who come to his aid; indeed he is powerful and mighty.**

According to these verses, the reasons for allowing fighting at this stage are threefold: (a) because fighting had already been initiated against Muslims by the pagan Meccans; (b) because Muslims had been harmed by the pagan Meccans and expelled from their homes; and (c) because the persecution of these early Muslims occurred merely on account of their religious belief and not on account of any wrongdoing on their part. Fighting (qital) in this verse is thus allowed in response to prior aggression by the Meccan polytheists and unambiguously defensive. Furthermore, the right to profess monotheism and to defend this right when it is violently opposed by others is affirmed in the verse.

A number of Quran commentators highlight the defensive nature of fighting in these verses on behalf of wronged Muslims and potentially on behalf of other monotheistic religious communities who are similarly persecuted for their faith. According to our early exegete from the eighth century, Muqatil ibn Sulayman, Quran 22:39 lifted the earlier prohibition against fighting and allowed Muslims to defend themselves against the harm inflicted on them by the pagan Meccans. Such harm included physical torture and verbal abuse as well as expulsion from their homes. The reason for the infliction of these aggressive acts was that the Muslims had publicly acknowledged their faith in God and affirmed his oneness. Muqatil understands Quran 22:40 to mean that if God had not restrained the hostile polytheists of Mecca through the agency of the Muslims, the polytheists would have gained the upper hand and killed the latter. Subsequently the monasteries and churches of the Christians, the synagogues of the Jews, and the mosques of the Muslims would all have been destroyed. These houses of worship—in which the name of God is mentioned profusely—are meant to be protected by Muslims, he says.

Some of the later commentators offer similar interpretations. In the late twelfth century, Fakhr al-Din al-Razi comments that these verses granted permission to Muslims during the Medinan period to fight those who aggressively opposed the right of "the people of religion" (*ahl al-din*; a reference to religious people in general, not only Muslims) to worship freely and construct their houses of worship. It is in this context, he continues, that the monasteries, churches, and synagogues are mentioned, even though they belong to non-Muslims, for they are dedicated to the worship of the one God and not of idols.

These interpretations point out that, according to the Quran, coming to the defense of other persecuted religious communities (mainly monotheists beside Muslims) and thus ensuring freedom of belief can also be a legitimate objective of the military jihad.

Is only defensive fighting allowed in the Quran?

According to the Quran, only defensive armed combat can be legitimate. In addition to Quran 22:39–40, there is another very important verse that makes clear the defensive nature of the military jihad. This verse is found in Quran 2:190 which states: **"Fight in the way of God those who fight you and do not commit aggression, for God does not love aggressors."** According to the commentators, this verse was revealed in

628. In this year, the Muslims wished to perform the lesser pilgrimage known as *umra* in Arabic. (Umra is a shortened form of the obligatory pilgrimage [known as *hajj* in Arabic] that can be carried out at any time of the year. Hajj is carried out only during the official pilgrimage season, which falls during the twelfth month of the Islamic calendar, called Dhu al-hijja). Quran 2:192 verse granted Muslims divine permission to defend themselves against attack by the pagan Meccans on the sacred grounds of the Kaba, something they were previously forbidden to do. (The Kaba, according to Islamic tradition, is the shrine built by Abraham and his son, Ishmael, in Mecca to which Muslims, if they are physically and financially capable, must make a pilgrimage at least once in their lives.)

More broadly, commentators understand Quran 2:190 as prohibiting Muslims from initiating fighting and granting them the right to defend themselves should they be attacked. This is so because God does not love "those who begin fighting, whether in sacred or non-sacred territory," according to an early commentary attributed to Ibn Abbas, a close associate of Muhammad. Mujahid ibn Jabr (d. 722), a very early exegete who lived during the Umayyad period (which lasted between 661 and 750 CE), very simply states that, according to this verse, one may not fight until the other side commences fighting—no ifs, ands, or buts.

A number of commentators after Mujahid continued to uphold this categorical Quranic prohibition against initiating fighting. Our late twelfth-century exegete Fakhr al-Din al-Razi makes it very plain in his Quran commentary that the divine command "Do not commit aggression!" in Quran 2:190 is directed at *actual, not potential*, combatants, meaning that the verse allows fighting only against those who have actually started to fight and not against those who are able and prepared to fight but have not yet resorted to violence.

Other commentators, such as al-Tabari from the ninth century, also say this verse forbids deliberately attacking traditional noncombatants or civilians who do not fight, such as women, children, the elderly, the sick, the disabled, serfs or agricultural laborers, monks, hermits, and other peaceful religious functionaries; to do so would constitute a clear act of aggression.

That Muslims may resort to fighting only when attacked first by a belligerent enemy is further made clear in Quran 9:12–13. These verses state:

If they break their pacts after having concluded them and revile your religion, then fight the leaders of unbelief. Will you not fight a people who violated their oaths and had intended to expel the Messenger and began [hostilities] against you the first time?

In their commentaries on these verses, premodern and modern exegetes stress without exception that the violation of pacts by the Meccan polytheists, their denigration of Islam, hostile intentions toward Muhammad, and their initial act of aggression toward Muslims had made fighting against them necessary. Our early exegete from the late seventh century, Mujahid ibn Jabr (d. 722), comments that these verses refer to the powerful Meccan tribe of Quraysh that had started the fight against the allies of Muhammad, culminating in the battle of Badr in 624. The late eighth-century exegete Muqatil ibn Sulayman similarly holds that these verses refer to the Quraysh who began hostilities at Badr against the Muslims. Later exegetes like al-Tabari, al-Wahidi, al-Razi, and al-Qurtubi offer similar interpretations. Al-Razi draws attention to the Arabic verb *badaukum* in Quran 9:13—which translates contextually in English as "they initiated hostilities against you [you plural]"—which, he says, establishes that the aggressor is without doubt the greater offender.

A minority of exegetes maintained that Quran 9:12–13 refer to the Treaty of Hudaybiyya, the terms of which were violated by the pagan Meccans in 630. This was a treaty signed between the pagan Meccans and Muhammad and his followers in 628, according to which there would be no fighting for ten years between the two parties and their allies. Shortly thereafter, one of the pagan Meccan tribes violated the treaty's terms by attacking a tribe allied with the Muslims—this is the act of aggression understood to be referenced in Quran 9:12–13 by a smaller group of commentators.

Another Quranic verse states that it is the duty of Muslims to defend those who are oppressed and who call out to them for help (4:75), except against a people with whom the Muslims have concluded a treaty (8:72).

All these verses taken together clearly establish that in the Quran, fighting is a defensive activity against an implacable enemy that initiates fighting against Muslims. Muslims may also fight to protect houses of worship belonging to other religious communities, especially the monotheistic Abrahamic ones, when they come under attack in Islamic lands. Furthermore, Muslims may fight to protect vulnerable, oppressed people who cry out to them for help. Therefore, the military jihad may be understood, first and foremost, as a *moral* enterprise that is undertaken for these just causes: (1) To protect the rights of those who wish to worship one God when that right is violently infringed upon by hostile forces. (2) To defend those who have been attacked wrongfully by an aggressive party and who are helpless before such violent onslaughts. Jihad in the Quran is *not* religious, sectarian warfare undertaken by Muslims to narrowly promote their interests over those of others. Contrary to widespread assumptions held by non-Muslims and even some Muslims as well, the Quran does *not* mandate fighting to spread the religion of Islam or to expand political territory belonging to Muslims. The only legitimate purpose in the Quran for fighting is to defend Muslims, their allies, and kindred religious communities when they are the victims of oppression and are targeted for hostile, violent action by an unrelenting enemy who rejects peaceful overtures. Fighting must be justified on such moral and just grounds.

Military activity for any other purpose is unjustified and unlawful, according to the Quran.

Is jihad in the Quran holy war?

The term "holy war" has no parallel in the Quran. The frequent, careless translation of jihad as "holy war" in English (and other Western languages) is inaccurate, especially on the basis of the Quran. The term "holy war" implies a battle waged in the name of a supreme being, usually to effect the forcible conversion of nonbelievers. It is a total, no-holds barred war intended to utterly destroy the enemy—men, women, and children—when they refuse to convert. Both objectives are doctrinally and morally unacceptable in Islam. In addition to the verses already discussed, which establish the military jihad as defensive in nature, a very important verse—Quran 2:256—further states clearly and without any ambiguity: **"There is no compulsion in religion."** Another verse (10:99) asks, **"As for you, will you force people to become believers?"** There is no scriptural basis, therefore, for waging war (or employing other means) to compel non-Muslims to accept Islam.

Simply put, the Quran does not allow Muslims to attack non-Muslims on account of the latter's religious beliefs. Nowhere is this made clearer than in Quran 60:7—9 which state:

Perhaps God will place affection between you and those who are your enemies for God is powerful and God is forgiving and merciful. God does not forbid you from being kind and equitable to those who have neither made war on you on account of your religion nor driven you from your homes; indeed God loves those who are just and fair. God forbids you however from making alliances with those who fight you on account of your religion and evict you from your homes and

who support [others] in driving you out. Those who take them as allies are wrong-doers.

These verses explicitly state that Muslims may fight only those who are hostile to them and who have persecuted them violently for their faith. Non-Muslims who live peacefully with them and display no hostility are to be treated kindly and fairly, regardless of what they choose to believe. This position is repeated by the major exegetes of the premodern period. Thus the well-known twelfth-century exegete al-Zamakhshari stressed that these verses require Muslims to treat non-Muslims justly and without oppression, which he describes as an excellent command. Later in the same century, al-Razi would remark that, according to these verses "kindness and charity are permissible between polytheists and Muslims," but he disallowed military alliances. The famous Andalusian exegete from the thirteenth century, al-Qurtubi (d. 1273), was the most explicit and most insistent in maintaining that the command contained in Quran 60:8 to be kind to those who had caused Muslims no harm was applicable to everyone who belonged in this category, regardless of their religious affiliation, and that the command was valid and binding for all times.

Can Muslims continue to fight when the enemy stops fighting and seeks peace?

No, they cannot. The Quran prohibits the continuation of fighting under such circumstances. This is made very clear in Quran 8:61—which we may call the quintessential "peace verse"—that states: "**And if they should incline to peace, then incline to it [yourself] and place your trust in God; for he is all-hearing and all-knowing.**" This verse creates a clear and absolute moral imperative for Muslims to abandon fighting when hostile enemy troops lay down their arms.

This message is also stressed in Quran 4:90, which states: "**If they hold themselves aloof from you and do not wage war against you and offer you peace, then God does not permit you any way against them.**"

These verses taken together categorically establish that fighting may continue only as long as the enemy engages in fighting and that Muslims must agree to peaceful arbitration when the other side seeks it. Such a position has nothing to do with the religious beliefs of adversaries but rather with their peaceful nature or lack thereof. In the case of the pagan Meccans who intended to wipe out the Muslims on the battlefield, the Quran exhorted the latter to fight back zealously. Under such circumstances, the Quran commanded Muslim warriors to "smite their necks" (47:4) and praised those "who kill and are killed" (9:111) in such a defensive enterprise. However, if the same enemy were to renounce its aggressive ways by laying down arms and seeking terms of peace instead, Quran 8:61 makes clear that fighting against them must cease. In general, peaceful people, regardless of their religious beliefs, cannot be attacked for any reason, as stressed in both Quran 4:90 and 60:7–9.

This perspective is the diametrical opposite of the holy war mentality. Such a mentality conceives of fighting as a cosmic, eternal duty carried out in the name of a deity who sanctions such warfare to impose on others a belief system or ideology, which alone is held to be valid. This is expressly forbidden in Quran 2:256 (also 10:99). In the ideology of holy war, the enemy has no rights; a holy war must be waged until the enemy submits to its ideology or is annihilated. This would include killing traditional noncombatants, such as women, children, and the elderly. In sharp contrast, the military jihad as depicted in the Quran is fought for the just cause of defending oneself and others against wrongful attack and not for the purpose of spreading Islam through military force. Fighting must come to an end when the opposing side lays down its arms— the directive is very clear. Peaceful people, regardless of their beliefs, cannot ever be militarily targeted. The desire for religious or ideological supremacy fuels holy war; the quest for justice is at the root of the military jihad in the Quran.

Are the peaceful verses in the Quran abrogated by the "sword verse?"

Quran 9:5, sometimes referred to as the "sword verse," states:

> **When the sacred months have lapsed, then slay the polytheists wherever you may find them. Seize them and encircle them and lie in wait for them. But if they repent and perform the prayer and give the zakat [obligatory alms], then let them go on their way, for God is forgiving and merciful.**

Contemporary polemical literature that discusses Quran 9:5—whether produced by Islamist militants or by Orientalists (certain Western academics who study and write on Islam for various ideological reasons) and Islamophobes (people who fear and hate Islam and Muslims)—often claims that there is a consensus among Muslim scholars on the abrogating status of Quran 9:5. They convey the impression that Quran 9:5, all by itself, has been universally understood by Muslims to abrogate (cancel/invalidate) the meanings and applications of numerous Quranic verses that call upon Muslims to establish kind and just relations with peaceful non-Muslims.

A survey of some of the most influential Quran commentaries of the premodern period easily disproves this assertion. For example, our celebrated late ninth-century commentator al-Tabari forcefully took issue with some of his predecessors who had stated that Quran 9:5 abrogates Quran 8:61. Quran 8:61 is the peacemaking verse that states: **"If they should incline to peace, you should also incline to peace."** Among al-Tabari's predecessors was a second-generation Muslim (known as a

Successor) called Qatada ibn Diama (d. 736). Qatada is said to have commented that every pact mentioned in the Quran and every truce concluded by Muslims with polytheists through which they entered peaceful relations with one another were to be understood as having been abrogated by Quran 9:5. For example, he understood Quran 9:5 to have abrogated Quran 47:4, which allows for prisoners of war to be released with or without ransom. Qatada had concluded darkly that by the revelation of Quran 9:5 God had commanded Muslims to fight non-Muslims in every situation until they said, "There is no god but God."

Al-Tabari took great exception to such views. He commented that Qatada's position cannot be supported on the basis of the Quran, the sunna, or reason. (The sunna refers to the practices and sayings of Muhammad). According to al-Tabari, Quran 9:5 has to do only with the Arab polytheists of seventh-century Mecca, whereas Quran 8:61 is understood to refer to the People of the Book (mainly Jews and Christians) who cannot be fought when they make peace with Muslims. Neither verse, he says, invalidates the injunction contained in the other since they concern different sets of people and different circumstances, and both therefore remain unabrogated. Al-Tabari also notes that there were early scholars, like al-Dahhak (d. 723) and al-Suddi (d. 745), who had maintained that Quran 9:5 itself had been abrogated by Quran 47:4, which allows for prisoners of war to be released from captivity. This was in direct contrast to the position espoused by Qatada.

Al-Tabari's was not a minority position. After him, the well-known exegetes al-Zamakhshari, al-Razi, and Ibn Kathir (d. 1373) all continued to assert that the "peace verse" (Quran 8:61) remained an unabrogated one and its meaning and ruling were not affected in any way by Quran 9:5. All these scholars stressed that the command contained in Quran 8:61 to engage in peacemaking, regardless of the religious beliefs of the parties concerned, was valid and binding for all time.

Al-Tabari was equally forceful in affirming the unabrogated status of Quran 60:7–8 against, once again, Qatada, who was of the opinion that Quran 9:5 had abrogated these verses as well. All the major exegetes after al-Tabari similarly upheld the unabrogated status of Quran 60:7–8. These verses command Muslims to be kind and fair to all those who are peaceful and cause them no harm, regardless of their religion.

Although it is found earlier, the term "sword verse" (*ayat al-sayf*) begins to be used for Quran 9:5 particularly by commentators during the Mamluk period (1250–1517). This was the period when the Islamic heartland was besieged by marauding Crusader armies who had started to arrive from Europe by the late eleventh century and by Mongol invaders who destroyed the city of Baghdad in 1258. Exegetes from before the Mamluk period—al-Tabari from the ninth century, al-Wahidi from the eleventh century, and al-Razi from the twelfth century, for example—do not use this term for the verse.

In his influential commentary, the fourteenth-century exegete Ibn Kathir referred to Quran 9:5 as the sword verse, after which it seems to have become more common. He also wrote a separate work in praise of the military jihad against the Crusaders who were ravaging the Syrian coast during his time. He warns that the Muslim polity must exercise great vigilance particularly along its coastal areas where they were most vulnerable to attacks by the Christian invaders. He reminds his readers of the atrocities committed by the Crusaders on capturing Jerusalem in 1099, when they massacred almost 70,000 "worshipful, abstemious, and humble Muslims." His use of the term "sword verse" for Quran 9:5 in his commentary indicates that he is deriving a general mandate from the verse, otherwise historically restricted to the pagan Meccans of the seventh century (without, however, considering it to be a verse that abrogates the "peace verse"). This general mandate would allow Muslims to fight in self-defense the vicious new aggressors of his time as the equivalent of the seventh-century Meccan polytheists. For Ibn Kathir, the existential threat faced by Muslims during the fourteenth century was comparable to that faced by Muslims in the seventh century. Repurposing Quran 9:5 as "the sword verse" allows Ibn Kathir to link the battles of his time to those fought during the Prophet's time and thereby similarly assured of success. This is meant to reassure the Muslims during this fraught period that they too will survive the Crusader onslaughts, as long as they fulfill their required role as defenders of Islamic lands.

Are Christians and Jews singled out for fighting in the Quran?

Many have claimed that a particular verse—Quran 9:29—is to be understood as granting permission to Muslims to fight in general the People of the Book (as mentioned, a reference mainly to Christians and Jews; also sometimes referred to as "scriptuaries" in this work) who refuse to accept Islam or to submit to Muslim political rule. The verse states:

> **Fight those who do not believe in God nor in the Last Day and do not forbid what God and His messenger have forbidden and do not follow the religion of truth** *from among those* **who were given the Book until they offer the jizya with [their] hands in humility** [italics added].

Jizya refers to a kind of poll tax (or head tax) levied on adult male scriptuaries (primarily Jews and Christians, but also extended in practice to Zoroastrians, Hindus, Buddhists, and others in the later period) who are financially capable of paying it in exchange for exemption from military service. If the men from these groups elected to serve in the army, they were not required to pay the jizya. The jizya was not strictly a poll/head tax since the poor, women, and minors did not pay it. Under the early Rightly-Guided Caliphs of the seventh century, poor Jews and Christians received stipends instead from the state treasury in Medina to support them financially. (The "Rightly Guided Caliphs" were the four men who, in succession, assumed leadership of the Muslim polity after the death of the Prophet: Abu Bakr, followed by Umar ibn al-Khattab, then Uthman ibn Affan, and finally Ali ibn Abi Talib. They ruled between 632 and 661.)

A survey of the commentary literature shows a discrepancy between early and late understandings of Quran 9:29 that is highly relevant to our discussion. Our very early exegete Mujahid ibn Jabr (d. 722), who lived during the Umayyad period in the late seventh and early eighth centuries, briefly remarks that this verse was revealed during the campaign of Tabuk undertaken by the Prophet in 630. Muhammad organized this military campaign when he learned that the Byzantines were assembling an army near Tabuk, a place in northwestern Arabia, in preparation for an attack. When the Muslims reached Tabuk, however, no combat took place; the Byzantine army did not materialize, and Muhammad returned to Medina shortly thereafter. Mujahid's commentary on this verse establishes that it referred to a specific historical incident and it did not apply in general to the People of the Book.

Exegetes after Mujahid, however, routinely identify the referents in this verse as Jews and Christians in general who are required pay the jizya to be protected by their Muslim rulers. Al-Tabari in the late ninth century acknowledges that the historical context for the revelation of this verse was a possible war with Byzantium and that Mujahid had pointed to the hostile Byzantine Christians as those intended in this verse. Al-Tabari, however, understood the verse as referring to Jews and Christians in general, making no distinction between hostile and peaceful factions among them. He also considers the requirement of paying the so-called poll tax a marker of their legal subjugation and general inferiority to Muslims. These views are consistently reproduced by a majority of later exegetes and jurists in their works. There are a few exceptions—the thirteenth-century Andalusian scholar al-Qurtubi, for example, criticized this understanding of Quran 9:29 and vigorously advocated the compassionate treatment of the People of the Book under the protection of Muslims.

If we return to the actual language of the verse, it is Mujahid's interpretation that appears to be the more credible. The verse, after all, does not refer to *all* the People of the Book. As my italicization in the verse highlights, it only refers to a faction from among the People of the Book who are clearly wrongdoers. "From among those who were given the Book" is the translation for the Arabic phrase *min alladhina utu al-kitab*. The preposition *min* is partitive—meaning that it refers to a part of the whole of something. The verse, therefore, must refer only to an erring faction among the People of the Book who do not follow their own religious tenets (that require belief in God and the Last Day), who do not forbid wrongdoing, and reject the truth. Only such wrongdoers who intend harm to Muslims can be fought.

This "partitive" meaning becomes obvious when we compare Quran 9:29 to an important cluster of verses taken from the ninth chapter as well. These verses (Quran 9:113–115) state:

> **Not all are alike from among the People of the Book; there are those who are upright, they recite the revelations of God all night long and they prostrate [in prayer]. They believe in God and the Last Day. They enjoin what is right and forbid what is wrong and hasten to do good works. They are in the ranks of the righteous. Of the good that they do, nothing will be rejected. God is well aware of those who do good.**

These verses unambiguously praise the righteous among the People of the Book who are worshipful and carry out good deeds; they clearly are not intended in Quran 9:29. Instead, their reward as upright and righteous Christians and Jews is promised in Quran 9:115 in the hereafter.

A wholesale denunciation of the People of the Book cannot be supported within the overall context of the Quran, which recognizes the piety and good works of faithful Christians and Jews. One of the most cited verses on interfaith relations is Quran 2:62 that states: **"Those who believe, those who are Jews and Christians and Sabeans, whoever believes in God and the Last Day and does good deeds, surely their reward is with their Lord, and no fear shall come upon them, neither shall they grieve"** (this verse is repeated almost verbatim in Quran 5:69). Elsewhere in the Quran, righteous Christians and Jews are described as constituting **"a moderate, balanced community"** (5:66) and being so honest that **"if you were to give them a coin for safekeeping, they would return it to you"** (3:75). Quran 7:159 refers to a contingent of righteous Jews who guide [others] to the truth and are just. When certain Jews and Christians fail to live up to the moral standards of their own faith traditions, however, the Quran criticizes them, sometimes severely, for their lack of righteousness and warns them of punishment in the next world (e.g., Quran 98:6). A holistic, cross-referential reading of the Quran with careful attention to the original Arabic allows us to credibly question and undermine interpretations that understand Quran 9:29 as containing a blanket condemnation of the People of the Book.

Many modern Muslim scholars readily reject some of the classical interpretations of Quran 9:29. The leading Egyptian scholar of international law Muhammad Talaat al-Ghunaimi, for example, affirms that the verse should be understood in its historical context as containing a specific reference to the Byzantine Christians of the time who were hostile to Muslims and not to the People of the Book in general. Before al-Ghunaimi, the famous Egyptian scholar and reformer Muhammad Abduh (d. 1905) had confirmed this understanding as a more credible interpretation of Quran 9:29 and rejected the interpretations of some of the premodern commentators as ahistorical and unsupported by the language of the text.

Does the Quran tell Muslims not to be friends with Jews and Christians?

One does hear this assertion, especially in polemical contexts. To support this position, Quran 5:51 is usually cited. This verse states: **"O those who believe, do not take Jews and Christians as** *awliya*; **they are awliya of one another."** I do not translate the Arabic word "awliya" because it is a polyvalent word, that is, it is a word that yields multiple meanings in different contexts. Depending on the context, awliya (singular: *wali*) can mean: "supporters," "helpers," "partners," "allies," "friends," "close associates," "patrons," and "clients," among others. We know that the Quran advocates kind and respectful relations with people—regardless of their religious affiliation—who are peaceful and willing to coexist with Muslims (Quran 60:8, 4:90, 8:61). The Jews and Christians referenced in Quran 5:51 must thus be those individuals or groups from these religious communities who are hostile toward Muslims.

This becomes clearer when we look at verse 57 from the same chapter (chapter five) that states: **"O those who believe, do not take those among the recipients of previous scripture who mock and ridicule your religion, nor the unbelievers as your awliya. You shall reverence God, if you are really believers."** Of course such individuals or groups cannot be trusted as "allies" and "supporters," especially in times of crises and wartime situations. Contextually, a more appropriate translation of awliya in both these verses is "military allies" and "protectors." Jews and Christians of the seventh century who were trustworthy allies in the common struggle against injustice and oppression did fight alongside the Prophet in his army.

The Quran in general counsels Muslims not to take as allies or protectors anyone who intends them harm, even if they are close relatives. Quran 9:23 states, **"Believers, do not take your fathers or your brothers as allies/protectors [awliya] if they prefer unbelief over faith. Those who take them as** allies/protectors are wrongdoers." Quran 58:22 furthermore states, "You will not find a people who believe in God and the Last Day harboring affection for those who oppose God and His Messenger, even if they are their fathers or their sons or their brothers or their kinfolk." These verses have, of course, not been understood as broadly advising Muslims to break off relations with their fathers and brothers (and other family members) in every time and place; rather, this advice applies to only those family members and relatives who are hostile toward Muslims and cause harm to the latter in specific circumstances. The general command in the Quran is to show kindness toward parents and relatives, even if they are unbelievers, as expressed in several verses (Quran 17:23–24, 29:8, 31:14–15, etc.). The maintenance of good family relations is a high priority within Islamic ethics.

It is worth emphasizing here that, according to the Quran, how Muslims should treat other people depends on *what they do* and not on *what they believe*. In other words, only people's actions that have consequences for others in the public sphere can be judged but not their privately-held beliefs and faith. The Quran warns that only God can make the final decision about the correctness of religious beliefs, and therefore such judgments should not exercise the human mind but rather be deferred to the next world (Quran 5:48, 9:106, 22:17, and others). Muslims may not belittle another's religion, even if it involves idol worship (Quran 6:108) and may engage in debates with non-Muslims but only with civility and respect (16:125, 29:46, 41:34).

Does the Quran support offensive military activity to spread Islam?

One verse that could be and has been understood by certain authorities as allowing fighting for the sake of Islam is Quran 8:39 that states: "And fight them until there is no more persecution/trials [*fitna*] and religion is entirely for God. But if

they cease, then indeed God sees what they do" (a very similar statement is found in Quran 2:193).

From the rich commentary literature on the Quran, we learn
that early scholars of the first and second centuries of Islam
(seventh and eighth centuries CE) understood the Arabic word
"fitna" in Quran 8:39 (as well as in Quran 2:193) to refer to the
"trials and persecution" visited upon the early Muslims by the
pagan Meccans. These scholars include the famous al-Hasan
al-Basri (d. 728) who commented that "fitna" refers to persecution and tribulations. According to this verse, fighting is legitimate when undertaken to defend oneself against oppression
and torture.

Another early scholar by the name of Urwa ibn al-Zubayr
(d. ca. 713) also interpreted "fitna" in Quran 8:39 to refer to
the trials and persecution faced by the early Muslims in Mecca
which were intended "to lure them away from God's religion."
He says that after the hijra (emigration) to Medina, Muslims
were given the divine command to fight the polytheists because they were persecuting Muslims and violently preventing
them from freely practicing their religion. According to
Urwa: "So that religion may be entirely for God" expresses
the purpose of this sanctioned fighting, which is to ensure the
free and unfettered practice of religion by Muslims without
persecution—and not for the purpose of spreading Islam.

However, after the eighth century, a majority of exegetes
preferred to understand "fitna" in Quran 8:39 as a reference to
polytheism that must be uprooted so that Islam may prevail.
The phrase "if they cease" in this verse is, therefore, understood by them to mean "cease to practice polytheism" and not
"cease to fight." This is, for example, al-Tabari's preferred understanding in the late ninth century, although he records the
early eighth-century scholar al-Hasan al-Basri's understanding
of "fitna" as "tribulations" and is aware that this is the general
meaning of the word. Al-Tabari also alludes to a group of
earlier exegetes who were of the view that the phrase "if they
cease" refers to pagan Arabs who desist *from fighting*, not from

polytheism. Al-Tabari disagrees with this position without of-
fering a rationale for doing so. Al-Tabari's interpretation of
"fitna" as "polytheism" was adopted by several exegetes after
him, an interpretation that—dangerously—allowed the military jihad to be waged for a religious/theological purpose
rather than strictly for self-defense against those who have
committed a prior act of aggression.

Many modern Muslim scholars, however, agree with the
interpretation of the early authorities. These modern scholars
reject the later understanding of "fitna" as "polytheism" as a
forced, theological (mis)interpretation that is not in accordance
with the general and obvious meaning of the term. Such an interpretation also violates the overall spirit of the Quran, they
maintain. Thus the Egyptian scholar Muhammad Abduh in the
late nineteenth century emphasized that both Quran 8:39 and
2:193 have to do specifically with the circumstances during the
Prophet's time when he and his Companions were subjected
to much hardship because they had publicly professed their
faith. (The term "Companions" refers to the close associates
and followers—male and female—of Muhammad after his call
to prophethood.) In both these verses, "fitna" refers to the persecution of the early Muslims by the Meccan polytheists; this
persecution was intended to force Muslims to abandon their
religious beliefs and worship. The phrase **"so that religion
may be for God**," which occurs in Quran 2:193, is compared to
"so that religion may be wholly for God" in Quran 8:39 and
understood to mean that an individual's religious allegiance
should be sincerely and wholly for the sake of God and not
motivated by the fear of any human being.

The believers of the seventh century had the right not to
be enticed away from their religion nor to be persecuted on
account of it, says Abduh. He reminds us that the historical
context must be kept in mind: Mecca at the time of the revelation of the Quran was the stronghold of polytheism and the
Kaba the storehouse of idols. While the polytheist was free
and unrestricted in the practice of his religion, the monotheist

believer was in a state of subjugation and oppression. If the polytheist were to refrain from fighting and violence, then hostility against him would also cease; aggression against him is carried out only to make him renounce his violent, oppressive ways and for no other reason, states Abduh. Fighting commanded in these verses was intended to put an end to this hardship and thus "to ensure freedom of religion," so that no one may be forced to abandon his or her religion and/or face persecution on account of it. This position, he comments, is in full conformity with Quran 2:256 which states: "There is no compulsion in religion." Abduh, like Urwa and al-Hasan al-Basri in the first and second centuries of Islam, thus does not understand this verse to contain a broad mandate to wage war so that Islam eventually replaces polytheism (and possibly, by extension, all other religions).

Is the military jihad a permanent religious obligation in the Quran?

During the Medinan period, when fighting was allowed for justified reasons and authorized by the Prophet as the legitimate head of state, it became a moral and religious obligation that no adult (male) believer of sound mind and body could shirk without justification (a few female Companions also fought in the early battles). This obligation is stated in Quran 2:216:

> Fighting has been prescribed for you [plural] even though you find it displeasing. Perhaps you dislike something in which there is good for you and perhaps you find pleasing that which causes you harm. But God knows and you do not.

It is not clear whether this Quranic verse imposed a permanent religious obligation to undertake the military jihad on Muslims of later generations. If we carry out a survey of Quran commentaries composed roughly between the eighth and twelfth centuries, we find that Quran 2:216 prompted discussion among the exegetes as to who exactly was being addressed in the Arabic second-person plural object suffix *kum*, for whom fighting has been prescribed. Early scholars from the seventh and eighth centuries, like Abd Allah ibn Umar (d. 693), Ata ibn Abi Rabah (d. 733), and Ibn Jurayj (d. 767) firmly maintained that the duty of fighting was imposed *on the Companions alone*. In other words, the military jihad was understood to be obligatory solely during the lifetime of the Prophet, specifically against the pagan Arabs who had attacked the Muslims, and this obligation was not understood to continue after his death.

Even as late as the eleventh century of the Common Era, scholars like the Quran exegete Ahmad al-Wahidi (d. 1076) continued to endorse this early position that fighting as a religiously prescribed duty applied only to the first generation of Muslims who were contemporaries of Muhammad and who were defending themselves against violent persecution by the Meccan polytheists. It is clear that for several centuries a substantial number of scholars were of the opinion that the duty of carrying out military jihad had lapsed after the time of the Prophet—this position cannot be dismissed as a negligible one in Islamic history. On the contrary, as our sources indicate, this remained a credible and dominant view subscribed to by many influential scholars in the premodern period (roughly until the twelfth century).

We start to detect a shift in this position by the late twelfth century/early thirteenth century in the writings of the well-known exegete al-Razi (d. 1210). He asserts in his commentary that despite what early scholars had said in regard to Quran 2:216, he prefers to understand the verse as imposing the duty of fighting on both those who were present at the time of its revelation and those who came later. Al-Razi is fully aware that he is going against the entrenched position of prominent authorities from the eighth century, like Ata ibn Abi Rabah, who had maintained that fighting as a religious obligation had lapsed after the time of the Prophet. The historical circumstances of his time—plagued by vulnerability to external enemies—very likely prompted al-Razi to adopt this line of reasoning. We must remember that the Third Crusade (1189–1192) as well as the Fourth Crusade (1202–1204) were launched during the period when al-Razi lived; military defense would probably have weighed heavily on the minds of scholars at this time.

After al-Razi, the late thirteenth-century scholar al-Qurtubi (d. 1273) subscribes to very similar views. In his case, his concern to establish fighting as a required duty on the basis of this verse is prompted by the precarious situation in which Muslims in al-Andalus (Muslim Spain) found themselves, facing the Christian armies descending from the north during the Spanish Reconquista. By the time we get to the fourteenth-century exegete Ibn Kathir during the tumultuous Mamluk period, it is all but a given that based on this verse, the military jihad is to be understood as a religious obligation imposed upon all adult Muslim men for all time. Writing against the backdrop of renewed Crusader attacks as well as the Mongol invasions of his time, Ibn Kathir stresses that Muslims must undertake the military jihad "in order to repel the harm inflicted by the enemy on Islamic realms." Failure to do so would allow the enemy to occupy the territory of Muslims, seize their wealth, and enslave their children, he warns.

The views of al-Razi, al-Qurtubi, and Ibn Kathir became well established in the later period, so much so that most Muslims today are not aware of this earlier school of thought that restricted the applicability of Quran 2:216 to the time of the Prophet and his Companions alone, a position that endured until the height of the Crusades.

What motivated the military conquests that took place after the death of Muhammad?

We do not fully understand the reasons for the onset of the conquests in the post-prophetic period. The conquests seem to have occurred rather spontaneously after the death of Muhammad without much planning, if any at all, by the government in Medina. In the modern period, we tend to think of governments as centralized structures exercising control in practically every sphere of public life. This would not have been true in seventh-century Medina. Government was decentralized, and the caliph did not necessarily have oversight over all the activities that took place in his realm or even in his name. Raiding and fighting were normal activities in pre-Islamic Arabia, and there is no doubt that the conquests represented a continuation of these activities.

When we look at some of the military commanders who led these campaigns, we note that they were frequently drawn from the pagan Meccan elite who embraced Islam practically at the last minute before the fall of Mecca in 630. Such leaders included Khalid ibn al-Walid (d. 642) and Amr ibn al-As (d. 664) who had fought on the Meccan side against the Muslims before their late conversions. Islam probably sat very lightly on them, and in all likelihood, they saw no reason to abandon their warring pursuits inherited from the pre-Islamic era. Historians like al-Baladhuri (d. 892) label the conquests *futuh* (literally openings) and not jihad. In his historical work detailing the conquests, al-Baladhuri barely mentions the caliph, conveying to us that the caliph had very little to do with the organization of the conquests. Later historians, like al-Tabari (who was also an exegete as we know), would see the hand of God in these conquests and glorify them as having facilitated the spread of Muslim rule. But this is an anachronistic view (that is to say, it projects back a situation that would not have been possible in an earlier historical period) and cannot be considered reflective of attitudes toward expansionist warfare in the first two centuries of Islam.

The existence of substantial numbers of people who did not believe that the Quran had imposed the military jihad as a religious obligation after the death of the Prophet casts strong doubt on the idea that the conquests were religiously motivated. There is no explicit Quranic directive that would require military conquests to be carried out either to spread Islam itself or extend Muslim rule. Instead, as established so far, fighting in the Quran is a defensive and limited activity undertaken only in response to an act of prior aggression. The Quran also unequivocally forbids compulsion in religious matters and condemns violence for the sake of material gain, regarding it as a feature of pre-Islamic life (4:94).

In line with these scriptural directives, a number of our sources inform us that some of the most pious among the earliest Muslims are on record as having been opposed to military expansionism. One of them was Abdullah ibn Umar, the son of the second caliph Umar under whose reign substantial conquests took place. Another early authority was the Successor Ata ibn Abi Rabah (from the second generation of Muslims), who had maintained firmly that the Quranic authorization to fight as a religious obligation was restricted to the time of the Prophet only. The Arab (rather than Muslim) conquests that broke out after the death of Muhammad are therefore better understood as a continuation of the pre-Islamic raiding campaigns (termed in Arabic *ghazawat*) motivated by worldly concerns for material gain and an inclination for military adventure on the part of some. Such motivations immediately disqualify such military enterprises from earning the label of a military jihad based on Quranic criteria. Clearly, further historical research needs to be carried out to determine comprehensively the nature of these conquests and the motivations behind them.

What does the Quran say about martyrdom?

Martyrdom in the Quran is at best an ambiguous and vague concept. The Arabic term used almost exclusively in non-Quranic sources to refer to a martyr, military or otherwise, is *shahid*. However this Arabic term does not occur in the Quran with this meaning. Shahid in the Quran refers specifically to a legal witness or eyewitness and is used for both God and humans in appropriate contexts (e.g., Quran 3:98, 6:19, 41:53). Similarly, the related term *shahada*, which has come to mean martyrdom, especially of the military kind, in non-Quranic texts, refers only to "witness/witnessing" in the Quran. Only in later extra-Quranic literature (hadith, biography of the Prophet, and commentary literature) does shahid acquire the specific meaning of "one who bears witness for the faith," particularly by laying down one's life through military and nonmilitary means. Quranic phrases commonly understood to refer to the military martyr include *man qutila fi sabil allah/alladhina qutilu fi sabil allah* (those who are slain in the path of God; see Quran 2:154, 3:169). These Quranic phrases are, however, ambiguous and do not in themselves clearly refer to death on the battlefield. Another concept of "selling" or "bartering" one's self or the life of this world for the hereafter (Quran 4:74; cf. 9:111) has been connected to the notion of martyrdom, but the connection itself is not explicit in the Quran.

Is the religious status of a military martyr higher than that of other Muslims?

The Quran does not state that the military martyr enjoys a special, exalted status compared to other pious Muslims, as is commonly assumed. This is a view that crystallizes in certain kinds of post-Quranic writings, but its origin is not found in the Quran itself. The fact that this is a post-Quranic development becomes clear when we look at the exegeses of a key verse—Quran 22:58—that deals with the status of the pious military martyr versus the pious believer who dies of natural causes.

Quran 22:58 verse states, **"Those who emigrated in the path of God and then were slain or died, God will provide handsome provisions for them; indeed God is the best of providers."** The late ninth-century commentator al-Tabari and other exegetes after him understand Quran 22:58 to refer specifically to the Meccan Emigrants (called *Muhajirun* in Arabic) and to the handsome reward promised them in the next world, regardless of how they died. The verse is understood in general to point to the greater status of the Emigrants in general compared to other early Muslims. It is worthy of note that this verse does not assign to the Emigrant martyred on the battlefield a higher status than the Emigrant who dies naturally. The common characteristic of the two is their act of emigration in the path of God, a difficult act motivated by faith that, undertaken with sincere intention, is worthy of generous reward in the next world. The implication of this verse is that the believer who is slain on the battlefield and the believer who dies peacefully in his or her bed are completely morally equivalent, the critical yardstick being the sincerity of their faith and not the manner of their dying.

In his commentary on Quran 22:58, the thirteenth-century Andalusian scholar al-Qurtubi draws our attention to the contested definitions of a martyr in the path of God. He acknowledges that this verse establishes the complete equality of status between the Emigrant slain on the battlefield and the Emigrant who dies in his/her bed. Nevertheless, some legal scholars went on to assert that the believer who is slain on the battlefield is morally more excellent than the believer who dies naturally. As a result, the *Sharia* (revealed ethics and law), as interpreted and applied by the jurists, came to reflect this point of view. However, al-Qurtubi points out, their view clearly contradicts not only this verse but also Quran 4:100, which speaks of the reward due to the Emigrant who dies on the way "to God and His apostle," as well as a number of hadiths that assert the absolute moral equivalence between the believer who dies a natural death and the believer who is slain on the battlefield. One such hadith is attributed to the well-known Companion Anas ibn Malik in which the Prophet states, "The one who is slain in the path of God and the one who dies of natural causes in the path of God are the equal of one another in regard to the blessings and reward [that they reap]."

This discussion of Quran 22:58 by the commentators is significant because it underscores the contested definitions of martyrdom through time and the higher religious status that was assigned to the military martyr in the later period, especially in legal circles. We can therefore conclude that the "cult" of military martyrdom that becomes evident in certain kinds of late, post-Quranic literature developed not because of the Quran but *in spite of it*. Such a development was, after all, in outright contradiction to Quran 22:58, which contains a transparent warning *against* the very construction of such a cult.

Is suicide permitted in the Quran?

Suicide is categorically forbidden in two verses in the Quran. The first is Quran 2:195, which states: **"Spend in the way of God and do not cast yourselves into destruction with your own hands."** The second is Quran 4:29 that states: **"Do not kill yourselves; indeed God is merciful towards you."** Both verses forbid the taking of one's own life.

Muslim scholars consider the willful taking of one's life to be a violation of a fundamental theological principle that God has the unique ability to give and take away life. This theological principle is derived from the following Quranic verses: **"He [God] brings forth life and causes death, and to Him you shall return"** (10:56); and **"Abraham said, 'My Lord is the one who brings forth life and causes death'** (2:258). In Islamic doctrine, suicide is considered a major sin that will be punished severely in the hereafter. In recognition of the enormity of the sin of suicide, jurists typically have not allowed regular funeral services to be held for the individual who takes his or her own life.

Is terrorism condoned in the Quran?

Terrorism means causing fear among the civilian population and using unjustified violence to bring about wanton destruction of life and property. All such acts are forbidden in the Quran (and in other Islamic texts). Each and every human life is considered to be utterly sacred in Islam. For example, Quran 6:151 says: **"Whether openly or secretly, do not take life, which God has made sacred, except for the sake of justice and the law. He has instructed you thus so that you may use reason."** Quran 5:32 states categorically: **"If anyone kills a person—unless it be for murder or for spreading mischief in the land—it would be as if he killed all humankind; and if any one saved a life, it would be as if he saved all of humankind."** According to the Quran, the intentional murder of human beings is a grave sin and a crime that merits punishment in this world and the next: **"Whoever kills a believer intentionally, his recompense is Hell, where he will reside for all eternity; God is angry with him and has cursed him and has prepared for him a great punishment"** (Quran 4:93).

The Quran also takes a dim view of warmongers and those who cause strife and corruption on earth (called *fasad* in Arabic), for which stern punishment is decreed (Quran 5:33–34). The Quran does allow Muslims to fight but only in self-defense after they have been attacked; initiation of aggressive activity is clearly forbidden (Quran 2:190). The Quran also warns against letting the desire for vengeance and anger get the better of oneself, even when one has genuine grievances. Quran 5:8 declares, **"O Believers, stand firmly for God and be just witnesses. Let not the hatred of a people cause you to swerve from justice; act justly—that is closer to piety. Reverence God; indeed God is aware of what you do"** (see also Quran 5:2).

An important verse—Quran 2:194—lays down the principle of proportionality: Muslims responding to an act of aggression can do so to the extent of the original attack and only to the extent of defeating the fighting forces. Proportionality in reacting to wrongdoing is similarly stressed in Quran 42:40, although believers are also encouraged to forgive and reconcile with the wrongdoer instead. Given this stress on proportionality, the slaughter of whole groups of populations that include civilians is impermissible in Islamic moral and legal thought. On the same grounds, the use of weapons of mass destruction that cannot discriminate between combatants and noncombatants and can cause massive destruction to property, livestock, and the environment would be prohibited.

Classical Muslim jurists used the Quranic verses just cited and relevant hadith to define the boundaries between legitimate and illegitimate violence and to prohibit what today we call terrorism. Terrorists, after all, have no regard for the principle of proportionality; their violent actions are based upon a no-holds barred, scorched-earth policy that intends to destroy all and everything in its wake. Such actions violate foundational moral and ethical principles in the Islamic tradition.

2

JIHAD IN THE HADITH LITERATURE

The hadith literature contains the sayings of Muhammad, as reported by his Companions, the name given to the women and men who were his closest associates. The Arabic word *hadith* literally means "speech," "a statement." These statements of the Prophet were circulated primarily in oral form in the first two centuries of Islam (seventh and eighth centuries CE), afterward they began to be written down in hadith collections. The term "hadith" is usually translated into English as "report" or "tradition."

After the Quran, the hadith literature is the second most important source of morality, ethics, and law in Islam. A related term is *sunna* which refers to the customs, practices, and statements of Muhammad; it is, therefore, a broader term than hadith. In addition to the hadith literature, details about the Prophet's actions can be derived from the biographical literature (known in Arabic as *sira*) and historical works. Stories recorded in biographical and historical works about Muhammad were, however, often based on hearsay and not rigorously checked for reliability or credibility. As a result, these sources are not regarded as "canonical," that is, as authoritative as the hadith literature.

At the same time, not all hadiths are considered equally reliable or sound, meaning that critical Muslim scholars doubted that some of them were actually uttered by the Prophet.

Scholars in the formative period of Islam were very concerned about establishing the reliability or soundness of hadiths. Some hadith collections are considered more trustworthy than others because the scholars who put them together applied rigorous criteria for determining the reliability of the statements attributed to Muhammad. These criteria included careful scrutiny of the chain of transmission of the hadith—this chain of transmission includes the names of those who narrated the hadith going back to the Prophet. Scrutiny of the chain was necessary so that the scholars could assess the moral and intellectual qualities of each transmitter of any given hadith. If transmitters were known to have grave character flaws and faulty memories and/or known for their partisan and biased viewpoints, their reports were devalued and often rejected. To a lesser extent, scholars also looked at the content of the hadith to evaluate whether the statement could have credibly been made by Muhammad. If the content blatantly contradicted established Islamic principles or was contrary to reason, it was often determined to be forged or fabricated and rejected by careful scholars.

In the field of hadith studies, there are three main categories of reports indicating different levels of reliability. The first category refers to "sound" hadiths, called *sahih* in Arabic. These are hadiths whose narrators—men and women—were deemed to be morally beyond reproach and blessed with retentive memories. Furthermore, the line of transmission of these reports go back to the Prophet without interruption, so that it could be reasonably assumed that each narrator had heard the report directly from the person before her in the chain until it reached Muhammad. Hearsay was not allowed; each person in the chain of transmission must have personally met the source he was reporting from.

The second category refers to "good" or "fair" hadiths, called *hasan* in Arabic. Good hadiths more or less met the stringent criteria for the sound hadiths, except that minor flaws were discovered in one or more transmitters of the hadith.

The third and final category refers to "weak" hadiths, termed *daif* in Arabic. These were reports whose chain of transmission included one or more narrators known to have possessed a faulty memory, or to have been dishonest, and/or regarding whom little or nothing is known. Missing links in the chain of transmission also render the hadith weak. Weak reports are not to be used as proof-texts, that is, texts that provide support for specific doctrinal positions and legal decisions.

Hadith works typically contain a section on jihad that mostly, but not exclusively, refers to armed combat. These sections frequently address the importance of the military jihad, sometimes in comparison with other praiseworthy activities. Some hadiths describe the merits (in Arabic *fadail*) of carrying out the military jihad, prescribe rules of conduct during armed combat, identify noncombatants, and deal with the status of and rewards for the martyr in the afterlife, both in military and nonmilitary contexts. Other hadiths indicate broader meanings for the term "jihad" and appear critical of the narrow understanding of jihad as primarily military activity.

A sampling of reports occurring in well-known Sunni collections of hadith that refer to jihad both in its combative and noncombative sense is offered in this chapter. There are separate Shii hadith works not discussed here; the military jihad is not equally stressed within them. Military activity was no longer considered permissible for the majority of the Shia after the ninth century when their rightful Imam or religious leader is understood to have disappeared but who is expected to return at the end of time.

What does "jihad" mean in the hadith literature?

Various meanings of "jihad" become clear when we look at hadith collections chronologically.

One of the oldest hadith collections we have was compiled by the early ninth-century Yemeni scholar Abd al-Razzaq al-Sanani (d. 827). Its title in Arabic is *al-Musannaf* (referring to hadiths arranged under specific topics). This work is earlier than the best-known and most highly regarded Sunni work of hadith, which was compiled by the celebrated scholar Muhammad al-Bukhari (d. 870). The *Musannaf* contains a number of reports that were not included in later works. Such reports, even if they are not considered normative (i.e., prescriptive or binding for the believer), are still valuable as historical sources since they contain useful information about early contested views regarding key topics within Islamic doctrine and thought.

Thus we find that the *Musannaf* includes certain reports that preserve an early, lively debate about what constitutes jihad that fell out of circulation in the later period. One such hadith relates that a man once came to the Prophet and told him: "I am a timid man; I cannot bear [the idea] of meeting the enemy." Muhammad replied, "Shall I not indicate to you a jihad in which there is no fighting?" When the man expressed eagerness, the Prophet continued: "The *hajj* [the full pilgrimage carried out during the prescribed season for it] and the *umra* [the shorter pilgrimage that may be carried out at any time] are obligatory for you." This hadith is highly significant because it informs us that, first of all, while the hajj and the umra are religiously required acts, the military jihad is not; second, jihad may be carried out in different ways; and third, it was neither shameful nor sinful for *a man* to avoid military activity if he had no desire or aptitude for it. It is worth noting here that this report occurs in a variant form in later hadith works counseling only *women* to substitute the pilgrimage for the military jihad. Comparing the early and late versions of this report indicates to us that in the later period the term "jihad" became reconceptualized as a reference to primarily military activity in which only (virile) men took part. In the earlier period, "jihad" was clearly a much broader term that referred to certain praiseworthy nonmilitary and military activities equally available to women and men.

Early hadith works also preserve reports which reveal that the phrase "in the path of God" or "for the sake of God" (*fi sabil allah*) had multiple meanings in the early centuries of Islam. (In the later period, this phrase was usually joined to the word "jihad" and mostly understood to be a reference to armed combat.) The multiple meanings of the phrase "in the path of God" are indicated in a noteworthy hadith recorded in Abd al-Razzaq's *al-Musannaf*. The report relates that a number of the Companions were sitting with Muhammad when a man of muscular build, apparently a pagan from the tribe of Quraysh, came into view. Some of those gathered exclaimed, "How strong this man looks! If only he would exert his strength in the way of God!" The Prophet asked, "Do you think only someone who is killed [in battle] is engaged in the way of God?" He continued, "Whoever goes out in the world seeking licit work to support his family is on the path of God; whoever goes out in the world seeking licit work to support himself is on the path of God. Whoever goes out seeking worldly gain has however gone down the path of the devil."

This report is noteworthy for two reasons. First, it contains a clear rebuke to those who would understand "striving in the way of God" only in military terms. It praises instead the daily struggle of humans to live their lives for the sake of God, which makes ordinary human activities, such as earning a livelihood, morally and spiritually significant and, therefore, worthy of divine approval. Second, the report emphasizes the importance of personal intention in determining the moral worth of an individual's act. Correct intention determines the moral value of an act, as stressed in the famous hadith: "Actions are judged by their intentions." Thus an act carried out for sheer material gain is not one that is carried out in the path of God. Since the meritorious nature of an individual's striving for the sake of God depends upon sincerity of intention, one may also understand this report as advising caution against accepting at face value showy, insincere acts of religiosity. It also warns against assuming that what appears to be a pious activity to humans—such as the claim to be waging a true military jihad—will be regarded as such by God, who alone can know the true intention of the individual.

The different meanings of jihad continue to be preserved in the famous hadith collection of al-Bukhari (d. 870). The title of this collection in Arabic is *al-Sahih*, indicating it contains only sound reports, as determined by al-Bukhari himself. Al-Bukhari is considered the most reliable compiler of hadith by the majority of Muslims who are Sunni. In his chapter on jihad, al-Bukhari records a hadith in which one of the Companions asked the Prophet which action is considered the best. He replied, "Prayer at its appointed time." When the Companion asked, "And then?" Muhammad replied, "Devotion to parents." The Prophet was once again asked, "And then?" to which he responded, "Jihad in the path of God." According to this report, obligatory acts of worship, like the daily prayers, and filial devotion to one's parents outweigh the military jihad in the path of God in moral value and priority.

The greater moral excellence of devotion to one's parents compared to the military jihad is stressed in another hadith which relates that a man came to Muhammad and asked his permission to take part in fighting. The Prophet asked, "Are your parents alive?" The man replied, "Yes." The Prophet advised, "Then strive [or do jihad] with regard to them." Here, "jihad" is clearly being used in the broadest sense of striving to do one's best in some praiseworthy activity, such as taking care of one's parents, and is deemed superior to armed combat in this context.

Another report stresses that carrying out the fundamental religious obligations within Islam is in itself highly meritorious and guarantees admission to paradise; taking part in the military jihad or not does not make a difference in this basic status. This hadith states, "God is obligated to cause whoever believes in God and His Messenger, performs the prayers, and fasts during Ramadan to enter paradise, whether he strove/ fought [*jāhada*] in the path of God or remained sedentary in the land he was born in." The same hadith, however, goes on to say that should such a pious person engage in the military jihad, then such an individual would attain a greater reward in the next world. This indicates that the legitimate military jihad is a meritorious voluntary activity for which the person who undertakes it earns extra merit, but it is by no means a religious requirement and makes no difference in one's basic status as a believer.

There are also reports that praise the military jihad when it is carried out with the proper intention and for a worthy purpose. One such hadith simply states: "Coming and going in the path of God [here "path of God" by itself appears to refer to military activity] is better than the world and what is in it." Another report declares that whoever is wounded in the path of God will be brought to life on the Day of Judgment "with the color of blood and breath of musk." These reports taken together convey a very high estimation of the military jihad but only when carried out with the right intention and for a noble cause, as signaled by the inclusion of the phrase "in the path of God."

A second well-known hadith collection was made by another esteemed scholar by the name of Muslim ibn Hajjaj (d. 875; also known simply as Muslim). His collection is also titled *al-Sahih*. This work is considered by Sunni Muslims to be second in status only to that of his contemporary al-Bukhari. Muslim ibn Hajjaj includes many of the hadiths recorded by al-Bukhari on various topics, including jihad, sometimes with different wording. He also included certain reports that al-Bukhari left out of his collection because they did not meet his more stringent criteria. One such hadith that was accepted by Muslim ibn Hajjaj but rejected by al-Bukhari quotes Muhammad as affirming three times that one is unable to perform a deed equivalent in merit to that of the one who fights in the path of God, even if one were to pray and fast all the time. Muslim acknowledges that versions of this hadith go back to a transmitter whose reputation was rather doubtful in the field of hadith transmission, and al-Bukhari did not accept reports transmitted solely by him. It should be noted that a number of hadiths that contain exaggerated praise for military activity were in fact regarded with suspicion by many scholars and not everyone accepted them, as in this case.

Another such report that attests to a higher status for the military warrior in a hierarchy of pious people is included by the late ninth-century hadith compiler al-Nasai (d. 915). According to this hadith, Muhammad is said to have guaranteed a house on the periphery and in the middle of paradise for those who had believed in his message, embraced Islam, and emigrated. But for those who had believed in him, embraced Islam, and "fought in the path of God," he vouchsafed not only a house in the periphery and the middle of paradise but also a house in its highest pavilions (*ghuraf*). In this hadith, the military jihad clearly trumps the *hijra* (emigration from Mecca to Medina), otherwise the central event in the inauguration of the Islamic era and the establishment of the Muslim community. Noteworthy also is the cooptation of the pavilions (*ghuraf*) of paradise in a military context. In the Quran, the heavenly pavilions are promised exclusively to the God fearing (Quran 39:20), the patiently forbearing (cf. Quran 25:75), and in general for those who believe and do good deeds (Quran 29:58). The transfer of this distinctive reward from the pious noncombatant believer to the pious combatant represents a stark subversion of the Quranic hierarchy of moral excellence. It should not surprise us that this report containing such exaggerated praise for the military jihad recorded by al-Nasai cannot be found in other authoritative collections of hadith.

Do hadiths describe how a military jihad should be carried out?

There are a number of reports that describe how a legitimate military jihad should be carried out. These reports stress that the true military jihad is one that is, first and foremost, carried out with correct intention and for a just purpose. For example,

Muslim ibn Hajjaj records a significant cluster of hadiths in which several Companions assert that there will always be "a group of Muslims fighting for the truth" until the Day of Judgment. hose who fight for personal glory and fame instead are destined for punishment in the next world. Other reports in Muslim's hadith collection emphasize just conduct during military combat, especially in relation to civilians. He lists noteworthy hadiths that forbid killing women and children during battles.

The hadith work of another important scholar from the ninth century, Ibn Maja al-Qazwini (d. 886), records several reports from the Prophet strongly prohibiting attacks against women and children. These prohibitions against killing women and children are repeated in practically every major hadith collection that includes a discussion of the military jihad.

There are additional hadiths recorded in the legal literature that offer more counsel regarding right and just conduct during battle, particularly concerning the treatment of civilians and protection of crops and property in enemy territory.

How should we understand the hadith that commands Muslims to fight non-Muslims until they accept Islam?

This hadith is frequently cited in certain quarters to establish the nature of jihad as religious warfare. The hadith quotes the Prophet as saying, "I have been commanded to fight people until they bear witness that there is no god but God and that Muhammad is the Messenger of God, perform the prayers, and offer the obligatory alms; if they were to do that, they would protect their blood and property from me, except for what is due on it to Islam, and their reckoning is with God." This hadith is recorded by al-Bukhari and Muslim and therefore meets the rigorous criteria of hadith analysis established by these two scholars.

Modern-day militants in particular cite this hadith to justify their violent campaigns against non-Muslims and against those they consider to be lukewarm or lapsed Muslims. One should note, however, that although al-Bukhari and Muslim included this hadith in their collections, not all scholars agree about the reliability or soundness of this report. The principal problem with this hadith is that its chain of transmission is characterized as *gharib* (literally "rare," "strange," "obscure"). The prominent hadith scholar and jurist of the ninth century Ahmad ibn Hanbal (d. 855) did not include this hadith in his collection. Another important hadith scholar from the fifteenth century, Ibn Hajar (d. 1449), recorded the names of several scholars who discredited the reliability of this hadith.

With regard to its interpretation, there is general agreement among Muslim scholars that the hadith refers specifically to the Arab polytheists of Mecca who had persecuted the early Muslims. Its content is, therefore, not applicable to the People of the Book or to non-Arab polytheists. The majority of jurists and exegetes have also maintained that an invitation to Islam must be carried out without coercion; this well-established principle is derived from the following Quranic verses: Quran 2:256 : "There is no compulsion in religion"; Quran 18:29: "Let him who wishes, believe, and let him who wishes, reject (it)"; and Quran 109:6: "You have your religion and I have mine." There is also Quran 60:8: "God does not forbid you from being kind to those who do not oppose you in religion." The hadith, therefore, should properly be understood as allowing Muslims during Muhammad's lifetime in the seventh century to fight back against the Meccan polytheists who had committed violence against them. Understood in this historical context, the hadith would not have any general applicability beyond the seventh century and cannot be used to justify forced conversion to Islam.

What does the hadith literature say about martyrdom?

The martyr is called *shahid* in the hadith literature. This is in contrast to the Quran, which uses the term "shahid" only in the sense of "a witness." The Quran, in fact, does not have a specific term to refer to martyrdom, military or otherwise.

Compared with later hadith collections, many of the reports contained in early hadith works preserve the broadest, noncombative meanings of the term "shahid." In one such report recorded in the *Musannaf* of Abd al-Razzaq, the shahid is described as one who dies in bed without sin and is thus entitled to enter heaven. Another noteworthy report states: "Every believer is a witness" (shahid) and references the Quranic verse "Those who believe in God and His messengers are the truthful ones and witnesses" (57:19). In these two reports, we have valuable testimony from an early source that the Quranic term "shahid" (and its plural *shuhada*) are to be understood as referring broadly to righteous believers who bear witness to the truth in the way they lead their lives and die peacefully in their beds. The term "shahid" in these texts does not refer to military martyrs, which became the common understanding in the later period.

Furthermore, several reports recorded in the *Musannaf* specifically challenge those who emphasize that martyrdom refers primarily to dying on the battlefield. In one such report, Muhammad is quoted as saying, "The one who dies [of natural causes] in the path of God is a martyr." Another report describes three kinds of martyrdom resulting from falling off a mountaintop, an attack by wild animals, and drowning at sea. A third report recorded in the *Musannaf* declares that that there are four types of martyrdom resulting from the plague, childbirth, drowning, and a stomach ailment. There is no mention of martyrdom being earned on account of dying on the battlefield in these early reports.

An early legal manual records similar reports. This is the famous work titled *al-Muwatta* (meaning "the Well-Trodden Path") by the legal scholar Malik ibn Anas (d. 795). One hadith recorded in the *Muwatta* gives multiple definitions of a martyr. According to this lengthy hadith, the Prophet identified seven kinds of martyrs, in addition to those who died from fighting in God's path.

He who dies as a victim of an epidemic is a martyr; he who dies from drowning is a martyr; he who dies from pleurisy is a martyr; he who dies from diarrhea is a martyr; he who dies by [being burned in] fire is a martyr; he who dies by being crushed by a falling dilapidated wall is a martyr; and the woman who dies giving birth is a martyr.

This report assigns martyrdom to the believer who suffers a painful death from a variety of grave illnesses, from a difficult labor in the case of women, or from falling victim to an unfortunate accident, in addition to dying on the battlefield.

Reports such as these found in early hadith works clearly demonstrate that martyrdom was understood very broadly in the early centuries of Islam, before the term was later appropriated to refer more narrowly to the military martyr.

This becomes evident when we move on to al-Bukhari's famed hadith collection, compiled in the last half of the ninth century. Al-Bukhari records more hadiths that contain enthusiastic praise of the military jihad and vivid descriptions of the rewards waiting for the military martyr in the afterlife. References to noncombative martyrdom and its virtues occur but are noticeably fewer in al-Bukhari's work. In one such hadith, Muhammad declares martyrs to be of five kinds: Those who die from the plague, from stomach ailments, from drowning, from being crushed to death (perhaps by a falling wall), and by suffering martyrdom in the path of God. (This hadith is very similar to the one recorded by Malik ibn Anas in his al-Muwatta.). In another report, the Prophet states: "The plague is [a source of] martyrdom for every Muslim."

But other hadiths in al-Bukhari's collection single out military martyrdom as worthy of special rewards in the hereafter. One hadith states that there is a "house of martyrs" that is the best and most excellent of dwellings in the hereafter. Another report says that only the military martyr among the pious will wish to return to earth and be killed repeatedly to continue to multiply the rewards in store for him in the hereafter.

In his hadith collection, Muslim ibn Hajjaj also records reports that offer broad definitions of a martyr comparable to those found in early hadith works. For example, one such hadith states that whoever asks God sincerely for martyrdom will be granted the status of a martyr, even if such an individual were to die in bed. Another hadith recorded by Muslim quotes the Prophet as saying that one who is slain on the battlefield, one who dies (of natural causes) in the path of God, one who succumbs to the plague, and one who dies from a stomach ailment make up "those who are killed in the path of God." A variant report adds the victim of drowning to this list.

The Quran uses the phrase "those who are killed in the path of God," which is often interpreted as a reference to battlefield martyrs. This hadith shows, however, that the Quranic phrase "those who are killed in the path of God" is to be interpreted more broadly to refer to those who died from a painful illness or calamity as well as on the battlefield. In qualifying for martyrdom, the phrase highlights the suffering of individuals rather than their manner of dying.

How can one know for sure that someone has attained martyrdom?

A number of reports in various hadith collections warn against attributing martyrdom to people on the basis of outward appearances and deeds. One such hadith relates that it was once mentioned before the Prophet that someone had achieved martyrdom. Muhammad remarked, "Not so. Indeed I saw him in a cloak which he had acquired dishonestly." The Prophet added that he would be punished in the hereafter instead. In another report, Muhammad stresses that "no one but a [true] believer will enter heaven." Reports such as this serve to check the rise of a potential cultic regard for what is deemed martyrdom. They emphasize instead the criterion of sincere faith

and righteous action in gauging true martyrdom, a determina-
tion that is beyond normal human ability.

As for the rewards the martyrs will enjoy in the hereafter,
many reports state that they include physical closeness to God
and the opportunity to engage in his praise. Their souls will
furthermore find pleasure in tasting the good things of paradise, including delicious fruit. This happy state will increase
when the souls are eventually reunited with their bodies. Some
reports say that the souls of martyrs will assume the form of
green birds who will flit about happily in paradise close to the
divine throne.

In summary, we may say that the rich hadith literature
attests that martyrdom was a broad concept in Islam's formative period that could be achieved in different ways. Peaceful
death in one's bed at the end of a life spent in devotion to God
and in the commission of good deeds was clearly the most general definition of martyrdom. Death from tragic suffering and
painful afflictions also conferred martyrdom. Other reports re-
late that martyrdom's best manifestation occurred on the battlefield when the believer waged war against the hostile enemy
and perished. Ultimately the hadith literature affirms that the
moral value of an individual's actions, which depends on the
sincerity of human intention, can only be judged by God who
alone is privy to such matters. Human assessments of such
acts are flawed and provisional at best.

Are there certain hadiths that appear to contradict the Quran on martyrdom?

Some hadith collections contain reports that glorify martyrdom excessively. For example, Abu Daud (d. 888) in his hadith compilation has a lengthy section on jihad in which the
bulk of the reports lists the merits (fadail) of the military jihad
and of military martyrdom. The tone of a number of these
reports is quite exaggerated in comparison with earlier hadith
works. One such hadith indicates to us a rising estimation of

the status of the military martyr in certain quarters. The report states that the Prophet made two men brothers; one of them was slain (it is assumed on the battlefield), while the other died (of natural causes) a week or so after the former. Several of the Companions prayed at the grave of the one who had died of natural causes. When Muhammad asked them what they had uttered, they replied that they had prayed for his forgiveness and implored that he would be united with his companion. At that the Prophet exclaimed that the prayers, the fasting, and the deeds of the two men in general were not comparable: "Indeed, [the difference] between them is like that between the sky and the earth!" This report conveys the view that the military martyr is vastly more morally excellent than the martyr who dies of natural causes.

The hadith gives us pause when we compare its content with that of Quran 22:58, in which the equal moral status of pious Muslims in this world and the hereafter is asserted, regardless of their manner of dying. This hadith clearly undermines the moral equivalence established by the Quran between the pious Muslim who dies peacefully in bed and the one who dies on the battlefield. Instead, this report recorded by Abu Daud grants a far superior status to the military martyr. The content of this hadith thus signals to us the rise of an excessive reverence for military martyrdom by the late ninth century among certain segments of the population This report is not found in al-Bukhari's and Muslim's collections: It was either not known to them because it was circulated in the period after them or it failed to meet their more rigorous criteria for the inclusion of hadiths.

Is there a hadith that promises the reward of seventy-two virgins to battlefield martyrs?

There is such a hadith. Its earliest version appears to be the one recorded by Abd al-Razzaq al-Sanani in his *Musannaf*. In this version, Muhammad promises nine distinctive rewards reserved for the military martyr: (1) forgiveness from God at the first drop of blood; (2) display of his seat in paradise; (3) decoration with the adornment of faith; (4) protection from the torments of the grave; (5) marriage with a dark-eyed woman; (6) safety from the "great terror" (of Judgement Day); (7) the placing of a crown of honor on his head, each sapphire in which is said to be better than the whole world and all that it contains; (8) marriage with seventy-two dark-eyed women; and (9) intercession in the next world on behalf of seventy of his relatives.

If we look at the chain of transmission of this hadith, we find that it consists primarily of Syrian transmitters of dubious reputation. For example, the Syrian transmitter Ismail ibn Ayyash (d. 798) was known for his prolific transmission of reports—"tens of thousands," according to one account—many of which were deemed to be weak as far as their reliability was concerned. Well-known scholars, like al-Bukhari, considered his reports to be particularly unreliable because Ismail ibn Ayyash would frequently doctor his texts and their chains of transmission. His so-called hadiths were deemed "obscure" or "strange" by scholars in Medina and Mecca and avoided by the Iraqis. Others declared that hadiths transmitted by Ismail could not be used as proof-texts. There are similar problems with other transmitters, also Syrian, who had related the report referring to seventy-two dark-eyed women.

The strong Syrian cast to this report is not unexpected in a report from this period praising the excellences of armed combat. Its exaggerated tone leads us to believe that it is promoting a controversial activity—fighting on behalf of the Umayyad rulers. It should be noted that the Umayyad rulers, who ruled between 661 and 750 CE, were highly unpopular with the general Muslim population, known as they were for their worldliness, impiety, and lukewarm adoption of Islam at best. Ratcheting up other-worldly benefits to enhance the lure of joining Umayyad armies, to put it rather bluntly, was a clever tactic under the circumstances. To find more recruits for their armies, which were frequently engaged in military skirmishes with the Byzantines, the Umayyad rulers promoted what has been described as a "jihad ideology," glorifying their military adventurism as fighting in the path of God. Circulation of reports praising military activity and promising the battlefield martyr generous rewards in the next world, including beautiful women, was very likely a strategy for inducing young men to join the Umayyad armies.

The inclusion of this report in Abd al-Razzaq's *Musannaf* indicates its early circulation but not its reliability. Neither al-Bukhari nor Muslim include it in their collections. Another well-regarded hadith scholar by the name of al-Tirmidhi (d. 892) does include a version of this hadith in his collection and classifies it as "good," "sound," and "rare." This classification indicates its restricted circulation in the early period despite what al-Tirmidhi deemed an acceptable chain of transmission.

Does the hadith literature encourage seeking martyrdom?

Like the Quran, the hadith literature does not encourage deliberately seeking death. Protection and preservation of one's life and those of others is the highest moral and ethical priority for a Muslim. There are hadiths that specifically warn against the deliberate courting of martyrdom by seeking to confront the enemy. One such hadith recorded by al-Bukhari relates that the Prophet during a military campaign would customarily wait until the sun had moved toward the West and then address his troops thus: "Do not wish to meet the enemy, O People, and ask forgiveness of God. When you meet them, be patiently forbearing and know that paradise lies below the shade of the swords."

Muslim ibn al-Hajjaj also records two hadiths that expressly forbid seeking to engage the enemy in battle. One of them quotes the Prophet as saying, "Do not wish to meet the enemy; when you meet them, be patient."

With regard to al-Bukhari's longer version of this hadith, it should be noted that modern militants typically like to quote only the last part of the report: "Paradise lies below the shade of the swords." Cut off from the rest of the hadith, this statement appears as an absolute endorsement of the military jihad and, therefore, may be understood as goading Muslims to deliberately seek military martyrdom. Reading this statement within the larger context of the full hadith conveys the exact opposite—the report counsels Muslims *not* to rush into fighting and *not* to court military martyrdom. If they are forced into battle by their enemies and consequently have to fight, they will reap their reward in the next world—but fighting in itself as flagged in this report as an undesirable activity that Muslims should not pursue.

Are there distinctly Shii views on martyrdom?

Because of the trajectory of Shii history, "redemptive suffering" and martyrdom, especially of the nonmilitary kind, loom large in the consciousness of the Shia and find plenty of reflection in their literature. From the perspective of the Twelver Shia (known as the Ithna Ashariyya or Imamiyya in Arabic—they are the majority of the population in Iran and Iraq), all twelve of their religious leaders (known as Imams) were martyred, starting with Ali ibn Abi Talib, the fourth Rightly-Guided Caliph, who was assassinated in 661. The battle of Karbala (fought in 680), in which al-Husayn, a grandson of the Prophet, and his family members were massacred by an Umayyad army, created a high degree of reverence for the idea of martyrdom among the Shia, especially in relation to the family of the Prophet. In the absence of their legitimate Imam (the last twelfth Imam is said to have disappeared from the world in 874), the military jihad lost its significance for a large majority of the Shia, and martyrdom was more a consequence of dying on account of suffering and persecution, rather than of military exploits on the battlefield. However,

after the Iranian Revolution in 1979 and during Iran's war
with Iraq in the 1980s, the notion of military martyrdom has
been used to mobilize the Iranian population against national
enemies.

What does the hadith literature say about suicide and terrorism?

Suicide is categorically forbidden according to a noteworthy
hadith recorded by al-Bukhari. In this hadith, the Prophet
refers to a man who had fought valiantly in a battle and
was wounded. But then he took his own life because he
could not stand the pain resulting from his injury, which
led Muhammad to remark that he would be punished in the
hereafter. Another frequently cited hadith states that a person
who takes his own life using an object or implement will be
repeatedly tormented by the same object in the next world—a
painful fate meant to convey the seriousness of the offense of
taking one's own life.

  As for terrorism, there are numerous hadiths and other
kinds of reports that assert that women, children, and other
noncombatants can never be targeted during a legitimate war.
Terrorists have no such regard for the boundaries of legitimate
violence and often deliberately target civilian populations,
seeking to sow fear and mayhem among them—activities
strongly condemned in both the Quran and the hadith literature. Jurists in their legal writings prescribed severe punishment for those who resorted to violence against civilians
through highway robbery, piracy, and other criminal acts that
disrupted the social order.

What are the greater and lesser jihads?

The greater and lesser jihads refer to "internal/spiritual
struggle" and "external/physical struggle" respectively.
They are mentioned in a well-known hadith, according to
which, after returning from a military campaign Muhammad

remarked to his Companions: "We have returned from the lesser jihad to the greater jihad, which is the striving of God's servants against their base desires."

This report is admittedly late (likely circulated after the ninth century) and cannot be found in the compilations of sound hadiths put together by al-Bukhari and Muslim. Some well-known later scholars like Ibn Taymiyya (d. 1328) and Ibn Hajar (d. 1449) regarded this hadith as either weak or fabricated. The report was included, however, in other hadith works and scholarly writings by the eleventh century.

The fact that this hadith was not recorded by al-Bukhari and Muslim tends to diminish its value and reliability for some Muslims. However, it would be a mistake to thereby conclude that the concepts of the greater and lesser jihad do not have earlier analogues or equivalents. The specific terminology used in the report may be of later origin, but the concepts themselves date from the very beginning of Islam. There is no doubt that the terms "greater jihad" and "lesser jihad" correspond to the Quranic terms *sabr* (patient forbearance) and *qital* (fighting) respectively. So although the formal classification of jihad into greater and lesser forms is a late one, the concepts of the internal, spiritual struggle and the external, physical struggle are derived from the Quran itself.

Do standard collections list hadiths that describe nonmilitary aspects of jihad?

Yes, they do—a number of hadiths included in such collections emphasize the importance of striving against the lower self that prods humans toward base desires and deeds. These reports, however, are often spread throughout these collections and not conveniently grouped into one section or under one heading, which is why they are sometimes overlooked. In ninth-century hadith collections belonging to the prominent scholars Ahmad ibn Hanbal (d. 855) and al-Tirmidhi (d. 892), one such hadith is recorded in which the Prophet states: "One who strives against one's [lower] self is a *mujahid*, that is, one who carries out jihad." Another report recorded by Muslim ibn Hajjaj similarly emphasizes this internal, spiritual aspect of human striving for the sake of God; it affirms: "Whoever strives [*jāhada*] with the heart is a believer." Three of the most authoritative Sunni hadith compilers from the ninth century—al-Bukhari, Muslim ibn Hajjaj, and al-Tirmidhi—record a report in which the Prophet declared that "those who help widows and the poor are like fighters in the path of God." These hadiths show that spiritual and noncombative aspects of jihad have existed simultaneously with combative ones. A number of these reports were later reproduced by moral theologians in works written to aid the moral and spiritual development of their readers. These reports also receive much prominence in the writings of mystical (Sufi) scholars.

One less well-known but nevertheless well-regarded hadith scholar al-Darimi (d. 869) records the following report in which the Prophet is asked, "Who is the best of people?" He replied, "One who lives long and does good deeds." This report may be understood to contain a rebuke directed at those who court death on the battlefield and thereby aspire to shorten their lives in hopes of being counted among the best of people as a military martyr.

In some collections of hadith and in works composed in praise of knowledge, striving to learn the Quran in particular and the pursuit of scholarship in general are also included as not only constituting jihad but also representing the best manifestation of it. Thus, al-Tirmidhi records the following frequently quoted report: "Whoever departs in the pursuit of knowledge is on the path of God until he returns."

A hadith recorded by the eleventh century Andalusian scholar Ibn Abd al-Barr (d. 1071) in his treatise on the excellences of knowledge, states: "The prophets are two ranks higher in excellence than the scholars while the scholars are a rank above the martyrs in excellence." In this report, scholarship ranks higher than armed combat as meritorious activity. One who failed to see that the pursuit of knowledge constituted jihad might be suspected of being deficient in knowledge and insight, remarks Ibn Abd al-Barr. A report similarly praising religious scholarship is attributed to the famed Companion Ibn Abbas. When Ibn Abbas was asked to comment on what constitutes jihad, he replied that the best act of jihad was the establishment of a mosque in which religious scholarship is pursued.

Since pursuing and acquiring knowledge was a component of jihad, one who died while so engaged was also considered a martyr. Ibn Abd al-Barr records a report that quotes the Prophet as saying, "When death overtakes the seeker of knowledge, he dies as a martyr." This is a noteworthy hadith that challenges an exclusively military understanding of martyrdom and underscores instead the self-sacrifice and heroic effort inherent in intellectual and rational pursuits, which upon death confer martyrdom.

Over time, these nonmilitant understandings of jihad became even more entrenched in certain circles. For example, the eleventh-century Andalusian scholar Ibn Hazm (d. 1064) affirmed a higher moral valuation of the defense of Islam through noncombative, verbal, and scholarly means over combative ones in his hierarchy of actions that qualify as meritorious striving in the path of God. Thus, he says, jihad is best exercised, in order of importance, through (1) inviting people to God by means of the tongue, (2) defending Islam through sound judgment and carefully considered opinions, and (3) through armed combat. With regard to the third type of jihad, Ibn Hazm states that this is its least important aspect. When we look at the Prophet himself, he says, we realize that the majority of his actions fall into the first two categories, and although he was the most courageous of all human beings, he engaged in little physical combat. Ibn Hazm's hierarchy affirms that the struggle of the learned in explaining and defending Islam through reasoned argument and scholarship can be considered far more meritorious than armed combat and represents a more faithful imitation of Muhammad's own actions.

3

JIHAD IN THE
LEGAL LITERATURE

Jurists, unlike Quran commentators, hadith scholars, and moral theologians, primarily dealt with jihad as one of the obligations of the Muslim ruler and the Muslim population in the context of external relations with non-Muslim polities. Within legal-administrative contexts, jihad is, therefore, necessarily military in nature.

The Quran and the sunna were not the only sources that jurists drew on in creating rules for the conduct of warfare. Local customary practices and practical worldly considerations frequently played an influential role. Jurists were mainly concerned with maximizing the welfare of the Muslim community and protecting its interests against hostile foreign entities. With this objective in mind, they sometimes devised legal strategies that qualified or even bypassed clear Quranic injunctions and Muhammad's established practices on issues of war and peace in specific historical contexts. They also had to devise rules of warfare with no historical precedent. As in the modern nation-state, the executive and judiciary branches of government were concerned with guaranteeing the security of the state and of all who lived within it, Muslim and non-Muslim, against outside aggression. This realist approach led to the emergence of distinctive—and contested—legal perspectives with respect to the state's role in the military jihad. Such perspectives must be understood within the specific historical and political circumstances in which they took shape.

How did Muslim jurists understand jihad?

In the premodern period, jurists dealt with jihad as military activity undertaken by the state to guard its frontiers against penetration by enemies and to ensure the security of its population. Their writings on the waging of war as a state activity reflected a hard-headed, pragmatic engagement with the realities of the outside world. Legal works in this context are typically concerned with topics such as the protocols of declaring war; bearing arms; division of the spoils of war; treatment of prisoners of war and their families; permissibility of attacking enemy combatants when they use Muslims, especially children, as human shields; treatment of civilians during warfare; cutting down trees in enemy territory; taxes to be levied on land; treatment of those who ask for safe conduct; imposition of the so-called poll tax (*jizya*); and other relevant issues concerning non-Muslims in their interactions with Muslims.

Muslim jurists were very concerned about setting boundaries between what they considered to be legitimate and illegitimate violence. As a result, they paid close attention to the issue of noncombatant immunity and the categories of people to be treated as civilians and thus protected from intentional harm during warfare. Deliberate targeting of civilians was an example of illegitimate violence that violated the command contained in Quran 2:190: "Do not commit aggression!" Jurists typically interpreted this verse as forbidding attacks on civilian noncombatants—those who do not or cannot take part in fighting. (Unlike several Quran commentators, most classical jurists did not understand this verse to prohibit categorically the initiation of war by Muslims.)

The early eighth-century Medinan jurist, Malik b. Anas (d. 795), explicitly prohibited the killing of women, children, elderly men, and Christian monks and hermits in their cells. Malik stressed that the property of religious functionaries, like monks and hermits, should be left intact since that was their sole means of livelihood. He also cites the hadith in which the Prophet forbade his troops to commit treachery and mutilation. Other hadiths in which Muhammad forbids the killing of noncombatants, particularly women and children, are recorded. Malik furthermore records the advice given by the first caliph Abu Bakr in 632 to one of his generals, "not to kill women, children, and the elderly" or to mutilate or commit treacherous actions. The general was also advised not to cut down fruit trees or burn houses and cornfields and to refrain from killing livestock. When encountering hermits in their monasteries, he and his army were commanded not to disturb them or destroy their dwellings. Malik further records a report from Umar ibn al-Khattab, the second caliph, in which he forbids the killing of the weak and the elderly, women, and children.

The influential ninth-century jurist al-Shafii (d. 820; after whom the Shafii school of law is named) similarly stipulated that women, children, and prisoners of war may never be put to death. He also forbade the torture or mutilation of enemy combatants, in accordance with the Prophet's prohibition against the gouging of eyes or amputation of limbs. Furthermore, al-Shafii prohibited the killing of birds and higher animals on the basis of a hadith. Other groups of people who are considered noncombatants by jurists are the elderly, serfs or agricultural laborers, slaves, the chronically ill, the blind and those who are disabled in general, and the insane.

These restrictions have continued to be repeated in legal manuals and treatises on warfare, forming an essential basis for rules of humane conduct during armed combat. A general immunity not to attack noncombatants was upheld by jurists through the centuries, but exceptions are sometimes noted. If the enemy uses women and children or Muslim prisoners as human shields, then an attack may be launched if there is no other recourse. If traditional noncombatants like women and monks resort to fighting, they are to be treated as combatants. Even in such cases, however, many jurists said that women should not be killed given the hadith in which Muhammad expresses great remorse over the corpse of a slain woman during a battle. Animals are not to be indiscriminately slaughtered, plants and trees should not be chopped down, and crops burned, except in retaliation for such prior enemy acts.

How is war declared and by whom according to jurists?

There is a juridical consensus that a legitimate military jihad can only be declared by the recognized head of state. In the early period, this was the caliph. In the later medieval period, this could be the sultan (local or regional ruler) as well. This was based on the precedent set by Muhammad after his emigration to Medina where he was recognized as the head of state by Muslims and non-Muslims and was able to go to war against the Meccan enemy on their behalf.

In the protocol of war that had developed by the ninth century, the jurists generally insisted that a public proclamation of war should be made by the ruler. According to the understanding of the classical jurists, such a proclamation consisted of inviting the enemy to accept Islam. The early Medinan jurist Malik ibn Anas was of the opinion that non-Muslims could not be fought until they had been summoned to Islam, regardless of which side initiated hostilities. The ninth-century jurist al-Shafii had also maintained that polytheists who had not previously heard of Islam could not be fought until they had been summoned to Islam. If anyone among them is killed before such a summons, then a blood-geld (financial compensation for the wrongful taking of life) must be paid.

A detailed protocol for proclaiming war is outlined by al-Sarakhsi (d. 1096), a well-known jurist from the eleventh century. This protocol is based on a hadith according to which

Muhammad is said to have dispatched one of his generals on a military campaign and advised him as follows:

> Do not fight them until you have summoned them. If they should refuse, then do not fight them until they initiate [hostilities]. If they should initiate [hostilities], then do not fight them until they kill someone from among you. Then show them that slain person and say to them, "Is there not a path to something better than this? For now God Almighty has guided you, which is better for you than anything else on which the sun rises and sets."

This hadith is recorded by al-Bukhari and Muslim and, therefore, regarded as reliable by the majority of Muslim scholars. The report is remarkable for its pacifist tone, which advocates not retaliation for an act of aggression but reasoning with the enemy to demonstrate instead the wisdom of renouncing violence and accepting God's guidance.

Two other protocols recorded by al-Sarakhsi allow initiating hostilities: One after a public proclamation of war has been made, and the other without such a proclamation. These two protocols must be considered to have developed late in response to Realpolitik, that is, in response to the political realities of the day rather than out of moral considerations. Such protocols, after all, specifically violate the nonaggression clause in Quran 2:190. The first protocol described in detail should be considered a genuinely archaic one because it is in accordance with Quranic directives that forbid Muslims from initiating attacks.

Can civilians ever be targeted during a military attack?

The overwhelming majority of hadiths that deal with conduct during warfare record Muhammad's strict prohibition against targeting and harming civilians, especially women, children, and the elderly. Jurists duly recorded these prohibitions in their writings to mandate humane treatment of noncombatants during unavoidable fighting.

There is, however, one hadith that some cite to make the case that civilians can potentially be targeted in a military attack. According to this hadith, the Prophet was once asked whether it was permissible to attack pagan Meccan soldiers at night when their women and children would be exposed to danger. The Prophet replied, "They [i.e., the women and children] are from them [i.e., the pagans]." This hadith is recorded by both al-Bukhari and Muslim and, therefore, deemed sound by their criteria.

On the surface, it seems the hadith grants permission to Muslim soldiers to attack women and children who cannot be distinguished from male combatants. Given the fact that more hadiths state the opposite—noncombatants must be identified as such and protected as much as possible—this report must be understood as referring to a situation in which, out of necessity, Muslim soldiers have to fight the enemy at nighttime when such distinctions cannot be strictly maintained. Jurists recognized the moral quandary of launching such attacks when the survival of Muslims was at stake—their counsel was to avoid civilian casualties as much as was feasible under the circumstances and attempt to target combatants only.

This hadith bears comparison with a report recorded by the early Kufan jurist and historian Ibrahim al-Fazari (d. 802) in his early treatise on international law. In this report, one of the Companions relates:

We went out on a military campaign with the Messenger of God, peace and blessings be upon him, and we were victorious over the polytheists. The people in their zeal killed even the children. When that reached the Prophet, peace and blessings be upon him, he said, "What is the state of people who are so overcome by killing that they

slay even children? Do not ever kill children; do not
ever kill children; do not ever kill children." Then a man
asked, "O Messenger of God, are they not the children of
polytheists?" He replied, "Are not the best among you
the children of polytheists?"

The protection afforded to noncombatants, here specifically
children, regardless of their religious ascription, is understood
to be absolute in this report. This report is regarded as "well-
known" and "well-attested" according to al-Fazari.

Comparing the two hadiths allows us to reconcile what
appears to be contradictory directives. Al-Fazari's report is
unequivocal in stating that children may never be deliberately targeted and harmed during hostilities. When weighed
against this general directive, the report found in al-Bukhari's
Sahih is more appropriately understood to refer only to exceptional circumstances, such as nighttime, when noncombatants
cannot be distinguished easily from combatants. This was
how the fifteenth-century hadith scholar Ibn Hajar (d.
1449) explained the hadith recorded by al-Bukhari. He did not
find it to be contradictory to other reports that categorically
stress the immunity of children and other noncombatants
during warfare.

How did jurists view martyrdom?

Given their concerns, jurists dealt primarily with the military
martyr. In contrast to the Quran and several hadiths that do not
rate death on the battlefield to be more meritorious than dying
of natural causes, jurists over time came to confer higher status
on the military martyr. This is indicated by the fact that special funerary practices developed for such a martyr. The jurists
determined that, contrary to the normal practice, the body of
the martyr who dies on the battlefield is not to be washed. If
the martyr was wounded on the battlefield and died later in
his home, then his body is to be washed. Martyrs are to be

buried in the clothes they fought in, but their weapons are to be removed. Most jurists were of the opinion that there was no need to say the funerary prayers over the martyr's body; the assumption was that all his sins had been forgiven and that he would ascend to heaven right away. Some jurists record that there were differences of legal opinion concerning the funerary practices that would apply to different types of martyrs; for example, one slain by brigands versus one slain by non-Muslims, or one who had perished on land versus one who was killed at sea.

How are prisoners of war to be treated?

There is a diversity of views on this topic. Positions taken by jurists in the premodern period are broken down according to the legal schools that became established by the tenth century. These principal legal schools are Hanafi (named after Abu Hanifa, d. 767); Maliki (named after Malik ibn Anas, d. 795); Shafii (named after al-Shafii, d. 820); and Hanbali (named after Ahmad ibn Hanbal, d. 855). Jurists from before the ninth century predated the legal schools and their affiliations are, therefore, not mentioned.

From the eighth century we have the two very important scholars—al-Hasan al-Basri (d. 728) and Ata b. Abi Rabah (d. 733)—who firmly maintained that "the prisoner of war should not be killed, but may be ransomed or set free by grace." They based their legal opinion on Quran 47:4, which states that prisoners of war should be set free outright or after a ransom has been paid. Their views are consistently repeated by later jurists, although they mostly disagreed with them. The famous Hanafi jurist Abu Yusuf (d. 798) was of the opinion that al-Hasan's and Ata's views on the issue of prisoners of war should be disregarded. Instead Abu Yusuf advocated that prisoners of war should be invited to embrace Islam or be killed, thus sharply deviating from the Quran's position on the treatment of them.

The late eighth-century jurist al-Shafii (d. 820) allowed for several different options in dealing with prisoners of war. He said that the caliph may choose to release them or ransom them for a sum of money or through the equal exchange of prisoners. Al-Shafii pointed to the example set by the Prophet when he ransomed prisoners after the battle of Badr in 624. But al-Shafii went on to say that the ruler also has the choice of enslaving them and treating them as part of the spoils of war. For adult males, the ruler can further exercise his discretion in either having them killed without mutilation or, in the case of idol worshipers, summoning them to Islam, and in the case of the People of the Book (primarily Jews and Christians but also Zoroastrians) accepting the jizya, or the so-called poll tax, from them.

The thirteenth-century Hanbali jurist Ibn Qudama's views are very similar to al-Shafii's; he adds that women and children can never be put to death, but they may be enslaved at the ruler's discretion.

The later Hanafi jurist al-Sarakhsi (d. 1096) indicates an early diversity of views on the issue of ransoming prisoners. He notes that eighth-century authorities like al-Hasan al-Basri and Ata ibn Abi Rabah continued the Prophet's practice of ransoming prisoners and were known to have been against killing prisoners on the basis of Quran 47:4. Al-Sarakhsi's views are much harsher, however, which he seeks to justify in the following way. He describes Hasan's and Ata's position as not worthy of consideration. Why? Because al-Sarakhsi considers Quran 47:4 to have been abrogated by Quran 9:5, which was revealed later. He acknowledges that Abu Hanifa, who lends his name to the Hanafi school to which al-Sarakhsi belonged , had commented that Quran 9:5 concerned only Arab idol worshipers and, therefore, was not applicable to the later period. Al-Sarakhsi dismisses this view as weak. The correct position, according to him, is that the option of releasing or ransoming prisoners had been abrogated and the ruler may not resort to either option, unless he is aware that there was general benefit in it for Muslims. Al-Sarakhsi emphasizes pragmatic and material considerations rather than scriptural and moral imperatives for adopting his harsher position vis-à-vis prisoners of war and disregards the well-established practices of the Prophet and early Muslims on this issue.

Comparison of early and later legal discourses on the treatment of prisoners of war is thus highly revealing of distinctive changes in attitudes toward them over time. These attitudes progressed from considerable leniency toward prisoners of war based particularly on Quran 47:4 in the early period to more draconian practices based on the individual preferences of the jurists and their functional concerns, even when such preferences departed from Quranic directives and Muhammad's own example. The reason appears to be that these later preferences were more closely aligned with the practices of war current among other cultures and nations during the time of these jurists.

Can Muslims fight under corrupt rulers?

One of the earliest jurists on record to grapple with this question is the eighth-century Medinan jurist Malik b. Anas. Our sources report that Malik initially expressed his distaste for the idea of fighting under corrupt and morally blameworthy rulers like the Umayyads. But he revised his opinion after the Byzantines attacked Marash and committed atrocities there. The city of Marash (called Germanikeia by the Byzantines and now called Kahramanmarash in Turkey) was destroyed by the Byzantine emperor Constantine V in 746. After this attack, Malik adopted the position that if fighting were to be abandoned under the Umayyad rulers in the face of aggression by hostile people like the Byzantines, untold harm to Muslims would result. For the greater common good, Muslims had to defend themselves against external aggressors under their rulers, regardless of their piety.

This became more or less the standard juridical position. Like Maliki jurists, Hanbali jurists also considered it permissible to campaign with corrupt leaders. Their view was that pragmatic and worldly considerations may influence one's decision to fight—or not—under a ruler. For example, it would be unadvisable to campaign with either the caliph or any ruler in the face of assured defeat and loss of Muslim lives. According to Ahmad ibn Hanbal, one should fight only with the commander who shows compassion for Muslims and takes due cautionary measures on their behalf. This is recommended even if he is known to drink wine, for traits such as these, says Ibn Hanbal, are merely personal failings and do not affect the general well-being of Muslims.

The duty to fight under one's rulers, regardless of their personal attributes, is thus regarded by most jurists as a pragmatic, functional one born of worldly concerns for security and self-defense against external aggression. In general, jurists were worried that if Muslims were to abandon fighting under corrupt rulers, there would be no one to defend their lands against an enemy who would come to rule over them and destroy their way of life.

Did jurists allow offensive military jihad?

Early jurists like Ata ibn Abi Rabah (d. 732) and Sufyan al-Thawri (d. 778) were firmly against the idea of offensive jihad. This was a position also upheld by a number of early exegetes like Mujahid ibn Jabr and Muqatil ibn Sulayman from the eighth century and later scholars like Fakhr al-Din al-Razi from the late twelfth century. These scholars resolutely maintained that Quran 2:190 was unambiguous in its prohibition of the initiation of armed combat by Muslims under any circumstance.

The influential jurist of the ninth century al-Shafii is said to have promoted the concept of offensive military jihad. He considered offensive jihad to be a collective duty and not an individual obligation. He classified it with the performance of funeral prayers rather than with the daily obligatory prayers, so that this collective duty is effectively discharged if there is a sufficient number of people undertaking it.

Building on al-Shafii's position, an eleventh-century jurist from the Shafii school, al-Mawardi (d. 1058), outlines what he understands to be a progressive Quranic articulation of the duty to fight, from its initial command to "turn away from the polytheists" (Quran 15:94), to summoning to God with wise counsel and gentle, respectful debate with the People of the Book (Quran 16:125), to fighting only those who initiate fighting with Muslims (Quran 22:39–40), and refraining from fighting those who do not resort to combat (Quran 2:190). Up to this point in time (until the battle of Badr in 624), the military jihad was not a mandatory obligation, says al-Mawardi. In his opinion, subsequent revelations, such as Quran 2:216, establish it as mandatory.

A very important question now comes to the fore for al-Mawardi: Can the Quranic verses permitting fighting be understood to allow all-out war, that is, equally against those who initiate fighting and those who do not? Al-Mawardi documents the view of Ata ibn Abi Rabah who asserted that it was *never* permissible to fight those who do not fight. Al-Mawardi takes exception to this view, stating that the doctrine of combative jihad reaches its final form in Quran 2:193, 9:5, and 2:191. In his understanding, these verses encode divine permission to fight equally those who fight and those who desist from fighting. The military jihad, argues al-Mawardi, had thus become a general obligation "in every time and place." Like al-Shafii before him, he regards it as a collective duty on the basis of Quran 9:41, which states: "Go out to battle lightly [armed] and heavily [armed]," as well as on the basis of Quran 9:122, which states: "The believers should not go out to fight altogether." The main purpose of the collective military jihad, he says, is to protect Islamic realms from the attacks of the enemy and thereby ensure the safety of the lives and property of Muslims. The military jihad is collectively obligatory only on free, adult, and sane males. If the enemy were to directly encroach upon Muslim territory and threaten it, then the collective duty of jihad becomes an individual one for all those capable of engaging in combat.

Like al-Mawardi, the eleventh-century Hanafi jurist al-Sarakhsi also outlines what he believes to be a progression within the Quran from forbearance and forgiveness toward polytheists to defensive fighting to offensive combat, which he declares to be "an enduring obligation until the Last Hour." The twelfth-century Andalusian Maliki jurist Ibn Rushd (d. 1198, known in the Latin West as Averroes) declared that all polytheists could be fought, with the exception of Turks and Ethiopians.

The thirteenth-century Hanbali jurist Ibn Qudama stated that the military jihad is an ongoing collective duty for those with the following seven characteristics: they are Muslim, post-pubescent, sane, free, male, free from physical defects, and financially solvent. Circumstances permitting, the military jihad should be carried out once a year by the ruler unless there is benefit for Muslims in not engaging in it or the Muslims are in a weak position.

This gradual watering down and then outright abrogation of the categorical Quranic prohibition against initiating fighting in later exegetical and legal literature can be understood as the triumph of political realism over scriptural directives. Political realism required that the Muslim ruler be allowed to launch preemptive wars to secure existing borders and expand territorial boundaries, in line with contemporary imperial practices in Byzantium and elsewhere. Jurists could sometimes be pressed into service to find the appropriate legal (and sometimes theological) rationale.

Given what we know of the political affiliations of a number of these jurists—both al-Shafii and al-Mawardi, for example, had close connections with the ruling Abbasid elite—we would be justified in saying that their interest in serving the cause of empire motivated them to radically reformulate the

Quranic concept of the military jihad. This tendency is quite prominent during the Abbasid period, but the trend had already started in the previous Umayyad period when a doctrine of aggressive warfare began to take shape. Such views became fairly commonplace in later juridical works, particularly during the Mamluk period when that part of the world we call the Middle East today was besieged by fierce Crusader and Mongol armies. Against this background, the fourteenth-century Shafii jurist Ahmad ibn al-Naqib al-Misri (d. 1368) in his legal manual, called in English translation *The Reliance of the Traveler*, would state matter-of-factly that one of the duties of the caliph was to declare war on non-Muslims. His assumption was that as non-Muslims, their hostility toward Muslims could be taken for granted. Such hostility, which could result in military aggression, should be preemptively neutralized.

There were however notable exceptions to this later trend, such as the twelfth-century scholar al-Razi, who was suspicious of extracting from scripture politically convenient interpretations contrary to the explicit, commonsense meaning of its text. Al-Razi maintained on the basis of Quran 2:190 that military activity could be launched by Muslims only against *actual*, not *potential*, combatants—a principled stand based on scripture that appears to have fallen out of favor to a considerable degree in administrative and legal circles in the late medieval period.

Did jurists consider the military jihad to be holy war?

It is clear from our sources that roughly by the early Abbasid period (mid-eighth century), the military aspect of jihad became foregrounded over nonmilitary dimensions, particularly in legal and administrative circles. Jihad from this period on would progressively be conflated with *qital* (fighting), collapsing the distinction that the Quran maintains between the two. As jurists and religious scholars of all stripes acquired considerable authority by the tenth century, they exercised the right to define the parameters of jihad and limit the range of activities prescribed by it. With the powerful theory of abrogation at their disposal, some (by no means all) jurists effectively rendered null and void the positive injunctions contained in Quranic verses that explicitly permit the conclusion of truces with foes and counsel coexistence with peaceful non-Muslims. These verses (e.g., Quran 60:8–9, 8:61) were understood to be abrogated, or at least superseded, by other verses, such as Quran 9:5, that give the command to fight. In the opinion of these jurists, this abrogation or supersession would remove scripture-based objections to the waging of offensive battles, not for forcing conversion, but to extend the political boundaries of Islam. Once conquered, non-Muslims were to be given the choice of either embracing Islam or paying the jizya. Usually acceptance of the second option (in the absence of the desire to convert) meant that the third option—"to be put to the sword"—devised by this camp of jurists for nonbelievers, would be infrequently exercised.

It would still be difficult to characterize offensive jihad of this sort as "holy war," mainly because these same jurists also upheld the principle of noncombatant immunity for women, children, the elderly, monks, and others who do not take part in fighting. This is not characteristic of a holy war, in which the demonized enemy has no rights, regardless of their combatant or noncombatant status. Instead of promoting holy war, these hawkish jurists could in fact be accused of doing just the opposite—that is, of politicizing and secularizing the military jihad so that it could be waged as "expansionist war." Such imperial wars of expansionism would further the state's objectives to expand territorially and extend its political dominion.

The politicization and secularization of the military jihad is apparent in the Arabic titles of works on international law (also called the law of nations), such as *Kitab al-jihad wa al-siyar*, which allowed for a religious concept (jihad) to be coupled with secular imperial law (siyar). This historical development was recognized by Majid Khadduri who stated:

> The transformation of Islam into a set of sovereign states brought in its train changes in the concept of the Islamic law of nations, produced by the new circumstances of life. First and foremost was the acceptance of the principle that the control of religious doctrines should be separated from that of external relations.

It should not surprise us that on account of the sensibilities of the day, politically motivated considerations had to be couched in religious rhetoric and theologically legitimized, a tendency that is not exactly unknown to us today.

Can women take part in the military jihad?

Women were present on the battlefield both during and after the time of Muhammad. Most were there for humanitarian reasons—they tended to the wounded and the sick, prepared food, and provided water for thirsty combatants. Aisha and Umm Salama, two of the Prophet's wives, are known to have accompanied him to battle. But a number of women took part in the actual fighting. Early biographical sources mention several of these martial women. One such female warrior was Umm Umara, a well-known woman Companion from the first century of Islam. According to one ninth-century Muslim biographer, she fought fearlessly in some of the early battles in Islamic history. During the battle of Uhud (in 625), she is said to have defended the Prophet himself against a particularly ruthless enemy and, consequently, was praised by him for her unusual bravery. That women should take part in the military jihad and related activities should not come as a surprise. The Quran (9:71) describes women and men as allies and partners (*awliya*) in the moral enterprise of commanding what is right and preventing what is wrong; defending oneself and one's community against military aggression would certainly qualify as such an activity.

Some of the later male jurists, however, were not enthusiastic about women's presence on the battlefield and tried to restrict this practice. The eleventh-century Shafii jurist, al-Mawardi, said they could be present but only for tending to the wounded and preparing food. Some said they should preferably be elderly. A major legal question arose as a consequence—did these women qualify for a share of the spoils of war along with the male combatants? Not surprisingly, there is a diversity of legal opinions on the subject.

According to the early Syrian jurist al-Awzai (d. 774), women present on the battlefield (whether as combatants or noncombatants) were to be given full shares equal to those allocated to male participants. Al-Awzai appealed to the practice of Muhammad, who had awarded full shares to women at the battle of Khaybar (629), for example. Such egalitarianism, however, was not to the liking of most male jurists after al-Awzai. Some of these later jurists said women could be given a small compensation rather than a full share, but others begrudged them even that much and said that they were not entitled to anything. Only the free, adult Muslim male is entitled to a full portion, they asserted, although they were fully aware of Muhammad's egalitarian practice and al-Awzai's juridical opinion based on it. One may reasonably conclude that these later juridical preferences were shaped by changing social attitudes toward the desirability of women's presence not only on the battlefield but, by extension, also in the broader public sphere. Clearly, after the early centuries of Islam, certain rights and privileges were being formulated in highly gendered terms to the detriment of women, even though these new formulations were contrary to the normative practices (sunna) of the Prophet.

Can Jews, Christians, and other non-Muslims take part in the military jihad?

Jews and Christians did take part in the military jihad along with Muslims, both during Muhammad's time and after. Historical and legal sources confirm that Jews and Christians took part in battles alongside the Prophet. Jews from the tribe of Qaynuqa, for example, fought with the Prophet in the military campaigns after Badr, for which they received shares equal to those of the Muslim soldiers. Muhammad also enlisted the help of Safwan, a pagan Meccan, during the battle of Hunayn fought in the year 630; for his help, Safwan was also given the full share of a Muslim.

As in the case of women, later jurists began to register their disapproval of such egalitarian practices in relation to non-Muslims. In his writings, the eighth-century jurist al-Shafii refers to the example of the Prophet who campaigned with non-Muslims and awarded them full shares. But his own opinion was that such practices should be discouraged because one cannot fully trust non-Muslims. Al-Shafii makes exceptions for situations in which they might prove useful to Muslims on account of their knowledge of enemy territory and military strategies. In such cases, he counseled that non-Muslims not be given a full share but only a small compensation or wage. Al-Shafii frankly acknowledges that his position is not based on the practices of Muhammad nor on those of his Companions but simply reflects his personal preference.

After al-Shafii this more or less became the standard juridical position. Even though later jurists acknowledged that Muhammad campaigned with non-Muslims and gave them full shares, they generally advised against the adoption of this prophetic practice. These changes in attitude and praxis allow us to conclude that a certain hardening of attitude toward non-Muslims occurred sometime in the late eighth century and gained momentum in later centuries, no doubt against the backdrop of hostile relations with non-Muslim polities and groups—with the Byzantines during the Umayyad and Abbasid periods, the Crusaders starting in the Seljuq period, and the Mongols during the Mamluk period. Realpolitik and hard-nosed self-interest rather than religious precedent drove these developments.

By the beginning of the ninth century, greater legal privileges were being conferred on the free, Muslim, adult male at the expense of women and non-Muslims. Even when Muhammad's own sunna was known to be contrary to such juridical practices, being besieged by ruthless enemies seems to have provided considerable sociopolitical impetus for abrogating earlier more egalitarian and magnanimous interpretations of the law.

Why did the medieval jurists divide the world into the Abode of Islam and Abode of War?

These divisions are said to have been created by early jurists from the Hanafi school of law (as mentioned, named after Abu Hanifa, d. 767) and further developed by the influential jurist al-Shafii in the late eighth-early ninth centuries. The Abode (literally House) of Islam, called *Dar al-Islam* in Arabic, referred to orderly Islamic realms in which the *Sharia* (revealed principles of law and ethics known from the Quran and sunna of the Prophet) was followed. The Abode of War, called *Dar al-Harb* in Arabic, referred to non-Muslim territories which were considered to be in a natural state of lawlessness and ipso facto opposed to the Abode of Islam. In al-Shafii's conceptualization, a third realm was added, called the Abode of Treaty (*Dar al-Ahd*) or the Abode of Reconciliation (*Dar al-sulh*), into which non-Islamic polities that had concluded peace treaties with Muslim rulers were admitted.

It should be noted that these concepts are not to be found either in the Quran or in the hadith literature. Rather they are the result of the jurists' independent reasoning, known in Arabic as *ijtihad*, and reflect the Realpolitik of their time. The study of law with the use of human reason is known in Arabic as *fiqh*, or Islamic jurisprudence. While the Sharia is known from divine revelation and regarded as perfect and infallible, fiqh is a human product that results from interpretations of the Sharia. Like all human products, fiqh is imperfect and changeable. When we refer to "Islamic Law" we are in fact referring mainly to fiqh, although many continue to use Sharia and fiqh interchangeably. One branch of fiqh, or jurisprudence, came to focus on the conduct of war by the state, which led to the development of the Islamic law of nations or international law, known in Arabic as *siyar*.

In the premodern world, Islamic international law was predicated on an existing state of "cold war" between territories inhabited by Muslims and those inhabited by non-Muslims, which required constant vigilance on the part of the former against the latter. In the premodern world, the default relationship among nations was, after all, war. Jurists, like the eleventh-century scholar al-Mawardi, acknowledged this historical reality and stipulated that one of the duties of the caliph was to carry out military campaigns against enemy territory at least once a year to expand Islamic realms and preempt potential attacks by their enemies. Other jurists were of the opinion that this duty could be fulfilled by simply being in an adequate state of military preparedness to forestall enemy attacks.

Al-Shafii's perspectives on jihad was, in many ways, a marked departure from earlier juristic thinking. This is quite evident when his views are compared with those of jurists from the earlier Hanafi school of law. Hanafi jurists did not subscribe to a third Abode of Treaty, as devised by al-Shafii. They thought the inhabitants of a territory that had concluded a truce with Muslims and paid tribute became part of the Abode of Islam and were entitled to the protection of the Muslim ruler. The early Hanafi jurists also held that nonbelievers could only be fought if they resorted to armed conflict and not on account of their unbelief, basing their position on Quranic injunctions. Their positions were undermined over time by jurists who went on to formulate a theory of offensive war based on political realism.

Does the division of the world into the Abode of Islam and Abode of War still apply in the modern period?

This binary vision of the world had already become passé by the twelfth century, as it no longer matched the political realities of the time. Muslim rulers frequently made treaties with non-Muslim rulers so that the "Abode of Treaty or Reconciliation" became a more meaningful category. Furthermore, the idea of a monolithic Abode of Islam seamlessly united against a monolithic Abode of War could not be maintained after the seventh century as Islamic realms splintered into different dynasties. The rulers of these autonomous dynasties were more likely to be warring among themselves than against external non-Muslim enemies. In the tenth century, there were three competing caliphates in the Islamic world—the Abbasid caliphate based in Baghdad; the Fatimid caliphate based in Cairo; and the Umayyad caliphate based in Cordoba, Spain, all at loggerheads with one another. Muslim rulers were not squeamish about allying themselves with non-Muslim rulers against a common enemy when it suited their purpose. For example, the Abbasid caliph Harun al-Rashid teamed up with the Holy Roman emperor Charlemagne in the ninth century against their common enemy, the Byzantines. The Ottoman Muslim rulers in the sixteenth century allied themselves with Francis I of France against their common rival, the Hapsburgs.

In the contemporary period, however, militant Islamists have resurrected the ninth-century concepts of opposed dual spheres or abodes , ignoring the period before the late eighth century (from the time of the earliest Muslims) when these notions had not existed, as well as the later period when these concepts fell into disuse. Although these divisions are not to be found either in the Quran or the sunna (a fact that may not be known to many among them), they promote these categories and the worldview behind them as required by Islam.

Most modern Muslim scholars tend to disregard this binary division of the world and dismiss it as an archaic, medieval *human* construct that has no relevance to the modern world. In the late nineteenth and twentieth centuries, the famous Egyptian reformers Muhammad Abduh and Rashid Rida recognized that this idea of a bipolar world had been defunct for centuries and explicitly affirmed that peaceful coexistence should be the normal state of affairs between Islamic and non-Islamic nations. Mahmud Shaltut (d. 1963), another Egyptian reformer who became the rector of al-Azhar University in Cairo, expressed a similar conviction. He stated that Muslims and non-Muslims were equal with regard to rights and duties in a Muslim-majority state and that only defensive wars were permissible in response to external aggression.

Did jurists permit suicide attacks?

Suicide is categorically forbidden in the Quran. The hadith literature also forbids the taking of one's own life and warns of punishment in the next world for those who do so. There is no scriptural basis for allowing suicide attacks of the type that one sees in the current period.

Jurists did ponder whether it was permissible to continue to fight on the battlefield when the odds were heavily against the Muslim army. In other words, they debated whether one could be morally justified in refusing to fight a superior army when that would lead to sure defeat and death. If a Muslim army determines that they would most certainly perish if they were to "patiently persevere" and fight against an army twice as large, can it retreat without intending to regroup or join forces with another contingent? The eleventh-century jurist al-Mawardi cites two competing views on this fraught subject: (a) the army may withdraw for God has counseled, "Do

not cast yourselves into destruction with your own hands"
(Quran 2:195); or (b) the army may not retreat, because in a
military jihad one either "kills or is killed," and by retreating,
the soldiers may fall into error. (In such a case, however, they
can compensate by resolving to regroup or join a fighting contingent.) Al-Mawardi concludes by affirming that "God knows
best," indicating that this is a perennial military dilemma to
which there is no easy, pat solution since the answer depends
on the specific circumstances in which such urgent decisions
must be made.

What are the views of jurists on terrorism?

The premodern, legal Arabic term that corresponds to our
modern understanding of terrorism is *hiraba*. The Quran
(5:33–34) describes those who generally wage war and cause
corruption on earth as carrying out hiraba, for which stern
punishment is prescribed. Jurists used the term "hiraba" to
designate specific activities like highway robbery, piracy, and
sedition, which sow fear among the civilian population and
create chaos and a feeling of helplessness in the public sphere.
This is very close to the modern definition of terrorism, a term
coined in English only in the twentieth century. According to
the Federal Bureau of Investigation (FBI) in the United States,
terrorism refers to "the unlawful use of force or violence
against persons or property to intimidate or coerce a government, the civilian population, or any segment thereof, in fur-
therance of political goals."

   This definition can be compared with the one given by the
Andalusian jurist Ibn Abd al-Barr (d. 1070) of the person who
carries out hiraba. He said: "Anyone who disturbs free passage in the streets and renders them unsafe to travel, striving to
spread corruption in the land by taking money, killing people
or violating what God has made it unlawful to violate is guilty
of hiraba . . . be he a Muslim or a non-Muslim, free or slave,
and whether he actually realizes his goal of taking money or

killing or not." Ibn Abd al-Barr's definition and that of the FBI both stress the unlawful use of violence and the spreading of fear among civilians; Ibn Abd al-Barr does not mention political goals in connection with hiraba for good reason. Political rebels were placed in a different category (*bughat*) by Muslim jurists for they were entitled to a fair hearing to determine whether their grievances were justified.

Terrorism is, therefore, unequivocally forbidden in Islamic law which holds human life and dignity to be sacred and inviolable, the protection of which is among its highest priorities. Twenty-first century militant groups like al-Qaeda, Boko Haram, and ISIS all qualify as terrorist groups, according to the definition of hiraba—they deliberately target civilian populations, and the propagation of chaos and fear in the public sphere is one of their prime objectives.

In 2014, over 120 Muslim jurists and scholars signed a letter denouncing the militant agenda of Abu Bakr al-Baghdadi, the so-called caliph of the "Islamic State of Iraq and Syria" (ISIS). The letter contains a long list of crimes committed by ISIS that are designated as terrorist activities. The consensus of these influential jurists places terrorist groups like ISIS outside of the Islamic mainstream. As some have argued, such groups should not be described as "jihadi" or "jihadist" for they clearly do not carry out jihad. Rather, they should be properly labeled as *muharibun*, that is, those who carry out hiraba, or terrorism.

4

JIHAD IN MORALLY EDIFYING, ETHICAL, AND MYSTICAL LITERATURE

By surveying a broader range of literary works, we gain a fuller sense of the various aspects of jihad. The typical focus on legal works in academic and popular discussions of jihad leads to overemphasizing its military dimension. There is another more important dimension of jihad represented by the Quranic trait called *sabr* in Arabic. I translate sabr as "patient forbearance," keeping in mind that this translation does not exhaust the range of meanings associated with the term.

Sabr represents the moral, spiritual, and social dimensions of jihad, so it is not surprising that we find few, if any, references to it in standard juridical works. In the hard-headed realms of international law and Realpolitik, legal works treat jihad as a state-sponsored military activity. Discussion of the merits (in Arabic, *fadail*) of cultivating patient forbearance as a necessary moral and psychological attribute of the pious individual belongs rather to the realm of religious ethics and social conduct. Patient forbearance (like other moral and ethical traits), after all, could neither be legislated nor enforced by the state. But moral and ethical treatises could and did focus on this essential trait for the believer. Sometimes this was a way for the writer to challenge an excessive focus on external and ritualistic expressions of religiosity at the expense of the internal and spiritual.

What does jihad mean in the daily life of the average believer?

While military jihad was regulated by the state, jihad, as it relates to the individual, is carried out through the conscious cultivation and practice of sabr in all aspects of life. The writings of moral theologians and ethicists that provide moral, ethical, and spiritual guidance focus on patient forbearance as the most important and enduring aspect of jihad. The cultivation of this trait is promoted as leading to numerous beneficial consequences for the purification of one's soul and mind; for establishing amicable and charitable relations with family members, relatives, neighbors, and others with whom one comes into contact; for proactively dealing with hostile and negative relationships and transforming them into positive, nurturing relationships; and for improving the self and the larger society. Sabr is the constant, defining attribute of the believer in any and every circumstance, which aids her in carrying out tasks from the simplest to the most demanding, in accordance with the interpreted divine will.

Sabr does not imply passivity or resignation in the Quranic context; sabr instead implies dogged fortitude in the face of life's many trials and tribulations. It also implies quietist (that is to say, nonphysical and noncombative) resistance to wrongdoing and evil. The Quran has a high regard for both quietist and activist resistance to wrongdoing, as expressed in Quran 16:110 and 47:31, for example. Patient forbearance in the Quran is intimately tied to jihad, broadly understood as the ongoing human struggle to promote what is right and noble and prevent what is wrong and degrading in all spheres of life.

Quran commentaries and edifying literature show that, in general, scholars understand sabr (and related words) to mean self-restraint and persistence in doing what is right and acceptable to God. The early scholar al-Hasan al-Basri (d. 728) said that sabr refers to steadfastness in performing the five daily prayers. His contemporary Ata b. Abi Rabah (d. 733) said that the related Arabic term *musabara* means to wait patiently for the fulfillment of the promise made to humans by God and not to give in to despair, waiting instead for deliverance and relief after hardship. Waiting for deliverance from hardship with patient forbearance is in itself considered to be an act of worship. The most common understanding of sabr is that it means to persist in acting contrary to the incitements of one's base, lower self, "for it beckons and one resists/should resist" when practicing patient forbearance.

A number of Quranic verses praise "those who practice patient forbearance" (al-sabirun); one particular verse—Quran 3:200—emphatically establishes the importance of this trait. It states: "O those who believe, be patient and forbearing, outdo others in forbearance, be firm, and revere God so that you may succeed."

The well-known Quran commentator from the late twelfth century, Fakhr al-Din al-Razi (d. 1210) eloquently describes the various aspects of patience indicated in this verse. Worldly life is composed of two spheres, he says: One has to do with the individual only, and the other is a collective space shared with others. In the first sphere, humans must practice patience and steadfastness in relation to themselves and their duties, while in the second they must practice patience and forbearance in their interactions with others. In the first individual sphere, patient forbearance is of various kinds. First, one must have patience in learning about differing viewpoints and complex proofs when acquiring knowledge of God's unity, about justice, prophecy, and resurrection, and in deriving firm conclusions from conflicting arguments. Second, one must have patience during the difficulties one faces in carrying out religious obligations and recommended actions. Third, one must be patient and steadfast in refraining from all prohibited things. Fourth, patient forbearance is to be exercised in the face of hardships in this world in the form of disease, poverty, hunger, and fear. God's command to exercise patient forbearance applies to all these categories.

In the second social sphere, a highly important aspect of sabr is the forbearance that one should display during unpleasant encounters with others, says al-Razi. This includes showing gentle forbearance toward members of one's family, neighbors, and relatives when they behave badly. The practice of patient forbearance also includes refraining from taking revenge on those who cause you harm, as counseled in Quran 7:199, "Hold to forgiveness, enjoin what is good, and turn away from the ignorant." Also relevant in this context is the verse, "When they pass by frivolity, they do so with dignity" (Quran 25:72). Further included in the practice of patient forbearance in the social sphere is showing a preference and love for the other over oneself, as mentioned in Quran 59:9: "They prefer [others] over themselves even when afflicted with poverty." This kind of patient forbearance practiced in the social sphere is called musabara in Arabic (as was also Ata's opinion). Musabara is derived from the same verbal root as sabr. This verbal form has the additional meaning of forgiving those who wrong you. Here al-Razi references Quran 2:237, which states, "Forgiveness is closer to God-conscious piety." The practice of musabara is clearly part of the larger moral enterprise of commanding good and preventing wrong. This is so because musabara involves showing forbearance toward the foolish when they are unable to understand what is right and true and engaging them patiently to help them overcome their inclination to falsehood.

Al-Razi warns, however, that even when practicing patience and forbearance, humans are still subject to the baser characteristics of their nature, such as anger, greed, and ignoble desires of all kinds that prompt them to act in foolish and immoral ways. Humans are engaged throughout their lives in striving to fight and overcome these base desires, which cause them to lose patience and abandon forbearance. In such contexts, Quran 3:200 becomes especially relevant, because it encourages believers to hold firm while engaged in this internal struggle. Those who refrain from giving in to their base desires and prevail over them are rewarded with success, he concludes.

Is the military jihad deemed to be the highest form of human struggle?

There is a common perception that the military jihad is regarded as the highest form of human struggle within Islamic thought. This cannot be supported if one turns to the Quran. The Quran actually says that those who practice patient forbearance in this world are the ones who will meet with the greatest divine favor in the hereafter. This is unambiguously expressed in Quran 39:10: "O my servants who believe—fear your Lord! For those who do good in this world is goodness and God's earth is wide. Indeed the patiently forbearing ones will be given their reward *without measure.*"

Italics are added in the translation, first to draw attention to the fact that there is no greater reward than "reward without measure" since it is without limit; and second, because this phrase occurs here only with respect to those who are patiently forbearing (*al-sabirun*). The same phrase "without measure" occurs in another Quranic verse (40:40) with regard to the reward in the hereafter that is promised to righteous men and women who do good on earth. The two verses taken together allow us to equate righteousness with the practice of patient forbearance and to appreciate the high valuation of sabr within Islamic morality and ethics. It is true that the Quran also speaks highly of "those who are slain in the path of God" who will be rewarded with paradise. We should recall, however, that the phrase "those who are slain in the path of God" is not understood to refer exclusively to the military martyr but rather to all those who have died after prolonged suffering due to various causes. This group of people, meritorious though they are, are not said to be rewarded without measure in the next world; this recognition is reserved only for those who are patiently forbearing and righteous. The famous late ninth-century exegete al-Tabari emphasized that Quran 39:10 promises that "the people of patient forbearance" will be given their reward without measure in the hereafter for what they endured in this world, meaning that there would be no "weighing and measuring" of the reward due to them.

So, historically, who were understood to be "the people of patient forbearance?" A few scholars understood this term to refer specifically to the first generation of Muslims who endured the hardships of the first emigration from Mecca to Abyssinia. This emigration to Abyssinia (current-day Ethiopia) by a small band of Muslims occurred roughly in 613 CE, encouraged by the Prophet. Ruled by the Negus, a Christian ruler, Abyssinia proved to be a hospitable refuge for the Arab monotheists, according to traditional sources. More frequently, scholars have understood this verse to be praising the Emigrants from Mecca to Medina for their patient forbearance during the trials they faced when making the difficult journey and for their continued suffering in exile. These early Muslims patiently bore the pain of separation from their homeland and their families and endured with great fortitude other trials and afflictions to safeguard their faith. As a result, they have been promised ample divine reward for remaining steadfast in their religion in spite of the persecution they faced for its sake. In one hadith, Muhammad says of them:

The scales will be raised and the people of alms will be brought forward and their compensation will be given with due measure. Likewise with [the people of] prayer and pilgrimage. Then the people who were afflicted with trials and suffering will be brought in and the scales will not be raised for them nor will their record [of deeds] be unfolded. Rather their reward will be heaped upon them without measure.

The report continues with the comment that upon seeing the magnitude of the reward bestowed on "the people of trials," those who had been spared such tribulations will wish that they had suffered a similar fate on earth.

Very similar interpretations of this verse are recorded by most commentators drawing attention to the great importance of cultivating patient forbearance as part of the daily ongoing human struggle (that is to say, of jihad) in this world.

What is the greater struggle?

The "greater struggle" (*al-jihad al-akbar*) is another name given to the "spiritual struggle" (*jihad al-nafs*). These terms are not found in the Quran; they occur in the hadith literature and in the writings of moral theologians in the premodern period. The Quran's term for "spiritual struggle" is sabr or patient forbearance. This Quranic virtue should be practiced in all spheres of life in order to resist the urgings of the lower, base self and to continue to grow morally and spiritually—this is, of course, jihad of the soul, pure and simple. This is why sabr is given the name of "spiritual struggle" or "the greater struggle" in later classifications or typologies of jihad. In these classifications the Quranic term *qital*, which refers to armed combat, is renamed "striving with the sword" (*jihad al-sayf*) or "the lesser struggle" (*al-jihad al-asghar*).

A clear Quranic pedigree can, therefore, be established for the concept of the greater, spiritual jihad under the term sabr. This kind of jihad predates the introduction of the combative jihad in the Quran after the emigration to Medina in 622 CE.

Why do some people resist the idea that the spiritual jihad is a genuine part of jihad?

In the West, a number of modern academics (by no means all), known as Orientalists, and certain pundits have resisted the idea that spiritual jihad is a genuine part of jihad. Orientalists are those Western academics who reduce Islam and Muslims to tired stereotypes and demeaningly portray Muslims as the civilizational "other." Pundits are public commentators and often self-styled Islam "experts" who, despite their shallow knowledge of Islam, are nevertheless influential in the way they shape public opinion in the West regarding Muslims. Both groups tend to maintain in a highly polemical vein that the concept of the greater spiritual jihad is a later construction and has no basis in the Quran. They further claim that it is an apologetic position adopted by Muslims (and their non-Muslim supporters) to "whitewash" Islam and "sanitize" the concept of jihad. This allows them to assert that authentic jihad is essentially violent in nature, and this is why Muslims are compelled to resort to violence in their interactions with the larger non-Muslim world.

To back these claims, these pundits and Orientalists typically make much of the fact that the frequently cited hadith in which Muhammad is quoted as saying after returning from a military campaign, "We have returned from the lesser [combative] jihad to the greater [non-combative and spiritual] jihad," is not to be found in the earliest sources. They point out (correctly) that this hadith is not recorded in the best-known hadith collections of al-Bukhari and Muslim ibn Hajjaj. They thus conclude that the concept of the internal, spiritual jihad cannot be authentically part of early Islam.

The fundamental error in this argument is the assumption that if certain terms appear late, then the concept within them could not have existed earlier, either without a specific name or under a different name. This is the error into which this group has fallen. The spiritual, moral, and social dimensions of jihad are all contained within the Quranic term sabr. Sabr is the earliest aspect of jihad in the Quran that was predominant during the Meccan phase of revelation and retained its significance during the Medinan period as an essential feature of human striving in the path of God. Although the terms "greater" and "lesser jihad" are post-Quranic and came into being roughly after the ninth century, there is no denying that the concept of spiritual and nonviolent jihad is firmly anchored in the Quran.

The term "greater jihad" (*al-jihad al-akbar*) itself may be understood to derive from Quran 25:52, which states: **"Do not obey the unbelievers and strive with it against them with a mighty striving (*jihadan kabiran*)."** There is an overwhelming consensus among commentators that God directs Muhammad in this verse to strive against untruth with the truths contained in the Quran. This kind of striving is considered by Muslim scholars to constitute "jihad of the tongue." The greater jihad is thus not only an internal individual struggle against one's base self but also an intellectual and discursive effort to challenge falsehood and oppression in the larger society and promote truth and justice in their place.

Framing the discussion of the internal, noncombative jihad in this larger context allows us to conclude the following: Whether the famous hadith that divides jihad into the greater, spiritual jihad and the lesser, physical jihad is reliable and a genuinely early report is irrelevant. What is relevant is that the concept of the internal, moral, spiritual and socially engaged jihad is without doubt Quranic in origin, although the terminology evolved and changed over time in certain kinds of literature. Those who are fixated on the dating of this report and its reliability—thinking they can thereby prove that jihad is authentically *only* a violent enterprise, while its spiritual and nonviolent dimensions are later, inauthentic developments—are missing this larger point.

We cannot be sure when the terms greater and lesser jihad gained prominence and began to displace the Quranic terms of sabr and qital in certain kinds of literature, especially mystical writings. Sabr continued to be used to refer to the spiritual jihad well into the late medieval period and has enjoyed a resurgence in modern writings.

Is the spiritual struggle carried out mainly by mystics?

The internal, spiritual jihad, signified by the Quranic term sabr, refers to the ongoing struggle on the part of all humans to control one's base desires and to strive to better oneself as an individual; this in turn is expected to lead to better relations with others. This broad understanding of the internal, spiritual, and social aspects of jihad lays to rest the assumption that you have to be a mystic to practice it. This is a claim made by some to downplay the central significance of patient forbearance or the internal, spiritual jihad in mainstream Muslim piety and ethics. It should be noted that Sufism or mysticism is not outside the mainstream of Islam; it is very much part and parcel of the rich mosaic of devotional practices and spiritual orientations that make up the diverse and dynamic Islamic tradition.

Are there references to nonmilitary forms of jihad in early Islamic writings?

We find descriptions of and praise for nonmilitary forms of jihad in the writings of a number of pious, learned Muslims from the formative period of Islam. One of our earliest surviving works on the merits (fadail) of practicing sabr (patient forbearance) dates from the ninth century. The author is Ibn Abi al-Dunya (d. 894), and the title of his work can be translated as *Patient Forbearance and the Rewards for It*. Renowned for his piety and humble lifestyle, Ibn Abi al-Dunya was a popular teacher and became the tutor of several Abbasid princes. He is said to have been the author of more than one hundred works, only roughly twenty of which have survived. He lived and died in Baghdad.

Patient Forbearance and the Rewards for It is a remarkable work for having preserved from a relatively early period hadiths as well as other reports not attributed to the Prophet, and various literary anecdotes, which praise the attribute of sabr as superior to other human qualities. In this work, patient forbearance is defined, above all, as an essential aspect of faith. The author preserves a quote from Ali ibn Abi Talib (d. 661, the Prophet's cousin and son-in-law who later became the fourth caliph after the death of Muhammad), which conveys to us the importance of cultivating patient forbearance as an essential moral and religious attribute. In this quote, Ali describes patient forbearance in its relation to faith as the relation of the individual's head to the body, with the implication that faith itself would be gravely diminished if patient forbearance were to be separated from it. Subsequently, Ali went even further and proclaimed that whoever lacks patient forbearance lacks faith.

The famous pious figure from the early eighth century, al-Hasan al-Basri, makes an appearance in this book and is said to have declared, "O humankind, do not cause harm; if you are harmed, be patiently forbearing!" Al-Hasan also considered those who suppressed their anger as practicing praiseworthy self-restraint and forbearance. The cultivation of sabr requires people to be nonconfrontational and non-vindictive in their interactions with those who wish to do them harm.

Since trials and tribulations are a constant fact of life, "the believer is in need of patient forbearance as much as he is in need of food and drink," says another authority cited by Ibn Abi al-Dunya. This perspective is affirmed in hadiths and other kinds of reports and anecdotes that point to the greater moral excellence of those who possess and display patient forbearance. One hadith is noteworthy for asserting the moral superiority of the patient, forbearing individual over all others, especially the military martyr. Ibn Abi al-Dunya quotes this report as follows:

> The Messenger of God, peace and blessings be upon him, wept and we asked him, "What has caused you to weep, O Messenger of God?" He replied, "I reflected on the last members of my community and the tribulations they will face. But the patiently forbearing from among them who arrives will be given the reward of two martyrs."

This report challenges other, better-known reports that assign the greatest merit to military martyrs and offers instead a different, non-martial understanding of virtuous self-sacrifice. The promise of a greater reward for patiently forbearing individuals in the next world is also a confirmation of their higher moral status in this world. Such reports in praise of patient forbearance are typically not found in the standard legal works or even in standard hadith collections, but in edifying literature, such as Ibn Abi al-Dunya's work under discussion here, which deals primarily with the ethical and spiritual formation of the believer.

How do Muslim mystics practice the internal, greater jihad?

Within the mystical strain of Islam known as Sufism, the Quranic trait of sabr assumes paramount importance. Muslim mystics do not typically withdraw from life or adopt celibacy like Christian mystics; family life and social engagement remain the norm for them. There is no monasticism in Islam. The lives of Muslim mystics are defined by the pronounced cultivation of an inner, spiritual life through contemplative practices and worship, in addition to carrying out the usual religious requirements of daily prayers, fasting, alms-giving, and discharging one's familial and social commitments.

One of the most important mystically-inclined scholars from the premodern period is the brilliant thinker Abu Hamid Muhammad al-Ghazali (d. 1111). He was born in Tus in northern Iran and received training as a conventional theologian. After being appointed to a prestigious academic position in Baghdad, al-Ghazali suffered the equivalent of a nervous breakdown at the height of his professional career when he was gripped by doubts concerning the value of purely academic scholarship. This triggered a lengthy spiritual odyssey, at the end of which al-Ghazali embraced the mystical, experiential path to God as being superior to other ways of seeking divine truth.

In his major work titled *The Revival of the Religious Sciences*, al-Ghazali includes a profound and moving chapter on the importance of cultivating the attributes of patient forbearance and gratitude to God that are intimately tied to one another. He says that faith in fact is composed of these two halves: patient forbearance and gratitude. One who is ignorant of the necessity of practicing patient forbearance and gratitude is thus ignorant of the two essential components of faith and consequently is deprived of the possibility of drawing close to God.

Al-Ghazali goes on to consider the importance of patient forbearance on its own. He stresses that over seventy verses in the Quran refer to sabr, its merits, and the reward earned by the believer for cultivating this trait. He refers to several of these Quranic verses as proof-texts to establish the excellence of patient forbearance. Verses that affirm that patient forbearance leads to positive consequences in this world and the next include Quran 7:137, which states, "Your Lord's fair word was fulfilled for the Children of Israel for what they had borne in patience, and we destroyed all that the Pharaoh and his people had done"; Quran 28:54, which states, "These will be given their reward twice over because they endure patiently and ward off evil with good and spend from what we provide"; and the well-known Quran 39:10, which states, "Those who are patiently forbearing will be given their reward without measure." This last verse, al-Ghazali explains, stresses that unlike other deeds and attributes which are rewarded according to a certain measure, patience and forbearance are not subjected to such limitations.

Patient forbearance is specifically a human attribute, continues al-Ghazali, denied to the animals on account of their deficient nature and to the angels on account of their perfection. Humans in their youth are like animals in that there is an excess of animal instincts at this stage and they lack patience. Through God's infinite mercy, two angels are sent to the individual at the beginning of puberty, "one of which guides him and the other strengthens him," thereby elevating humans from the level of animals. Then there starts a fierce struggle in the human soul between the "army" championing base, animal instincts on one side and the "army" fighting on behalf of religious piety on the other. Patient forbearance, our author asserts, is required in the successful waging of "war" by the "troops" of religiosity against those championing base desires.

The explicitly martial vocabulary used by al-Ghazali in his description of this fundamental spiritual struggle in the human soul is purposefully quite vivid and dramatic. It serves to highlight his conscious adoption of militant vocabulary in order to subvert the conventional meanings attached to jihad by jurists and others. The external battle between the forces of good and evil has been completely internalized by al-Ghazali and transferred to the "battle-ground" of the human heart.

Al-Ghazali singles out patient endurance of the harm inflicted by other people as "one of the highest levels of patience." He quotes from the Christian gospels as follows: "Jesus, the son of Mary, upon him be peace, said, 'It was said to you before—a tooth for a tooth, a nose for a nose, but I say to you, do not return evil with evil but rather to the one who strikes your right cheek turn to him the left cheek, and whoever takes your cloak, give him your shawl.'" This statement, al-Ghazali comments, enjoins patient forbearance in the face of injury by others. Such forbearance is deemed great because it is exercised in the face of one's competing spiritual and animal instincts, along with the anger that is provoked on such occasions.

Not surprisingly, al-Ghazali takes particular note of Quran 3:200. He says this verse has been explained to mean, "Be patiently forbearing *for the sake of* God, be patiently forbearing *through* God, and be firm with them *with* God." He understands the verse to counsel the constant cultivation and practice of patience, fortitude, and forbearance—the various aspects of sabr.

Did jurists refer to the spiritual jihad in their writings?

As is to be expected, jurists in their legal writings primarily focused on jihad as a state-mandated military duty for the Muslim collective, since that is the proper concern of public and international law. But some jurists also wrote on moral and theological issues; in such writings, they focused on the nonlegal sphere and wrote on topics that had to do with self-improvement and cultivating proper relations with God and one's fellow human beings. Among such authors is the well-known fourteenth-century Damascene Hanbali jurist Ibn Qayyim al-Jawziyya (d. 1350), who studied with another well-known fourteenth-century Hanbali jurist Ibn Taymiyya (d. 1328). Ibn Qayyim's legal thought remains particularly popular in Wahhabi and so-called Salafi circles today, but his theological and spiritual writings remain less well known.

One work written by Ibn Qayyim is an extended eulogy for the attribute of patient forbearance whose cultivation is deemed essential for the spiritual flourishing of human beings. The work's Arabic title can be translated into English as *The Preparation of the Patiently Forbearing Ones and Treasures of the Grateful Ones*.

Ibn Qayyim begins by emphasizing the centrality of patient forbearance in the Quranic discourse on personal piety and social ethics. He says:

Indeed God the exalted has made patient forbearance (sabr) like a race-horse which never stumbles and like a sharp sword which never misses its target. It is like an army which never suffers defeat, and like a formidable fortress is fortified against destruction and collapse. Victory and patient forbearance are full-blooded siblings, for victory goes along with patient forbearance as relief with distress, and hardship with ease. It is by far the most helpful [attribute] for those who possess it. Its position in relation to success is that of the head to the body,

for the All-Truthful, All-Trustworthy One in the clear
verses of the Quran has guaranteed for those endowed
with patience the awarding of their recompense without
measure.

The martial language of the first part of this passage reminds
us of al-Ghazali's language in reference to the conflicted
human soul. Once again, such martial imagery should not
come as a surprise to us when viewed within the larger sociopolitical context of such works. In this work, Ibn Qayyim, like
al-Ghazali, also understands the highest form of jihad to be the
cultivation of patient forbearance in all aspects of one's life, for
which there is boundless reward in the hereafter. He, therefore,
borrows the idiom of military jihad to express the intensity of
the spiritual struggle within the human soul that results from
the effort to cultivate patient forbearance. The adoption of this
martial language to describe the role of sabr in the daily life of
the individual is meant to challenge others who understand
the military jihad to be superior to the spiritual jihad.

In his writings, Ibn Qayyim does not devalue the external,
combative jihad when and where there is a need for it and
regards it as a highly meritorious, albeit conditional, act in
specific contexts. However, like al-Ghazali, he regards sabr as
trumping all other traits and considers its practice to be the
best of all deeds under *all* circumstances. Basing his views on
the Quran, he regards the relentless internal human struggle
to be patiently enduring of life's trials and tribulations as the
highest and constant feature of jihad on earth.

Not surprisingly, Ibn Qayyim, like al-Ghazali and others before him, takes special note of Quran 3:200 and singles it out
for an extended commentary. Ibn Qayyim comments that the
verse commands believers to be patient in themselves, to be
forbearing with others, especially those who wish them harm,
and to be firm and resolute (in Arabic rabitu) in their adherence
to patience and forbearance. He observes that the verb rabitu

and its corresponding verbal noun *ribat* or *murabata* have come to mean physically guarding the frontier territories on horseback to prevent attacks by enemy troops. This is a later martial meaning attached by some commentators to Quran 3:200, even though it is widely known to be a Meccan verse when there was no fighting. Ibn Qayyim asserts that in its own revelatory context, this highly significant Quranic verse means instead to guard the frontiers of the heart so that base desires and the devil cannot enter it. One may make a specific equation between the resoluteness practiced by the patiently forbearing individual and the resoluteness displayed by the warrior patrolling the borders in the post-prophetic period. Both, he says, play an essential role in warding off internal and external enemies that cause havoc to the proper ordering of life.

It should be noted that early Islamic sources confirm Ibn Qayyim's understanding of the Arabic verb rabitu that occurs in Quran 3:200. The verb rabitu yields the Arabic verbal noun ribat that in the later period acquires the secondary meaning of military patrolling of border areas on horseback. In its original Quranic context, however, the verb and its corresponding noun are understood by early scholars to refer to being steadfast in the carrying out of essential religious duties, particularly the daily prayers. Muslim ibn Hajjaj records a hadith in which the Prophet repeatedly affirms that waiting patiently to perform the prayers, one after the other, is called ribat. This is in contrast to later scholars, like al-Zamakhshari (d. 1144), who although aware that Quran 3:200 was a Meccan verse, still preferred to understand it in a combative sense. No doubt, such scholars wished to attach a lofty Quranic pedigree to the later military activity that came to be known as ribat to grant it additional moral luster.

For Ibn Qayyim, as for many others, jihad in a holistic sense is constantly carried out in the spiritual, moral, ethical, social, and intellectual realms of earthly human existence and only conditionally on the battlefield.

5

JIHAD AS CONCEIVED
BY MODERN POLITICAL
REVOLUTIONARIES
AND MILITANTS

It is hard to miss the rise of political revolutionary movements and militant groups in the Muslim-majority world in recent history. The global media profusely reports on their activities, and the internet provides abundant information on their ideologies and various agendas. Such groups did not arise in a vacuum, and their arrival on the world stage needs to be contextualized.

This takes us back to the eighteenth century when Islamic revivalist movements began to take shape in the shadow of increasing European encroachment on Muslim territories. Revivalist movements gained steam through the height of Western colonialism in the mid-nineteenth and early twentieth centuries and continued into the postcolonial period starting roughly in the mid-twentieth century. Dramatic changes in the social and cultural fabric of Muslim-majority societies during these periods evoked strong and varied reactions among a number of Muslim scholars, thinkers, and activists. The abolition of the caliphate by Republican Turks in 1924 created a deep political and psychological crisis in the Muslim-majority world. Attempts to revive the institution would follow. The emergence of Islamist political parties in the first half of the twentieth century was, in many ways, a reaction to this political vacuum. Such parties promised freedom and social justice to those who were politically and socially marginalized in their societies, framing such goals within an Islamic vocabulary of reform and egalitarianism. In 1928 the Muslim Brotherhood was established in Egypt to mount a campaign of reform against what was described as the materialism and secularism of its day. Above all, it sought to politically empower ordinary Egyptian people against what was regarded as a corrupt ruling elite that did the bidding of Western governments.

Not everyone was attracted to this kind of political revolutionary rhetoric. But—as with communism and other utopian movements—the ideal society promised by Islamism or political Islam was appealing to those who lived under repressive governments that had come into existence in many Muslim-majority countries at the end of the European colonial period. Many of these postcolonial governments were decidedly secular and were regarded by the local populations as serving the interests of an imperialist West rather than of the local populations. The memory of the humiliations that had been visited on Muslim peoples by European Christian colonizers remained strong throughout the twentieth century and hardened the resolve of the political revolutionaries that such indignities should not be repeated in the future. The creation of the Jewish state of Israel in 1948 by Western powers on what for centuries had been predominantly Arab land resulted in the displacement of hundreds of thousands of Palestinians. This was a painful and poignant reminder of the political powerlessness of Muslims on a global scale. The 1967 and 1973 Arab-Israeli wars resulted in the loss of even more Arab land to the Zionist state, further aggravating the Palestinian refugee problem and creating more grievances in their aftermath.

The dark memories of European colonial occupation were revived in the late twentieth and early twenty-first centuries by fresh Western, primarily American, incursions into the Middle

East during the first and second Gulf wars (between 1990–1991 and 2003–2011 respectively). American (and European) support for authoritarian governments in the Middle East and elsewhere in the Muslim-majority world continue to fuel dismay and disillusionment with Western governments and their local proxies. Under such disquieting and crisis-ridden circumstances, calls for revolutionary armed struggle against all regimes regarded as oppressive fall on many receptive ears. In the post–September 11 world, such calls have become more strident in some quarters, and violent groups now command the world stage with their militant rhetoric and tactics of terror.

How do modern militants in the Islamic world understand jihad?

In the early twentieth century the combative jihad began to be increasingly understood by militant Islamists as a means of bringing about sociopolitical reform in Muslim-majority societies through the removal—by violent or other means—of indigenous authoritarian, secular governments. This is a new dimension to jihad not encountered in the premodern period and is the child of modern nationalist agendas.

More recently, global militant groups have tended to think of jihad as a cosmic (universal) battle that must be waged until the end of time in which only one side—right-thinking Muslims who constitute the righteous camp favored by God (i.e., mainly themselves)—will triumph over others, namely, mainstream Muslims and non-Muslims. Many of these groups see themselves as fighting a defensive jihad in retaliation against all the wrongs, real and perceived, that have been done to them by others.

Which early thinkers influenced modern political revolutionaries and militants?

One of the earliest and most influential figures is the eighteenth-century Hanbali preacher and revolutionary Muhammad ibn

Abd al-Wahhab (d. 1792) from what is now Saudi Arabia. The ideology he founded is referred to as Wahhabism in English. As a young man, Ibn Abd al-Wahhab traveled to Medina where he studied under a teacher by the name of Abd Allah al-Najdi, who interpreted Hanbali legal thought very conservatively. From Medina, Ibn Abd al-Wahhab traveled to Iraq, Iran, Syria, and Egypt for further study. It was during this phase of his life that he began increasingly to engage in religious missionary and political activities, and he became critical of Sufi practices and Shii beliefs that he considered unorthodox. He aspired to establish a theocratic state governed according to what he understood to be Islamic principles. By 1744, he had taken up residence in Dariyya (near modern-day Riyadh) where he lived, preached, and taught until his death. It was here that he concluded an oath of mutual loyalty with a tribal chieftain by the name of Muhammad ibn Saud (d. 1765) to work together to establish a state based on Wahhabi principles; this state was eventually established as the Kingdom of Saudi Arabia in the twentieth century.

Ibn Abd al-Wahhab's strongly dogmatic and polemical views on many theological and legal issues earned him enemies during his lifetime; among them, apparently, his own father and brother. His views remain politically influential, primarily in Saudi Arabia and the Persian Gulf states, although zealous and wealthy Wahhabi missionaries continue to attempt to spread their message elsewhere in the Sunni Muslim world and beyond.

Ibn Abd al-Wahhab considered the general Muslim populace ignorant of the authentic teachings of Islam. In his opinion, this had led to confusion and unawareness about their own religious tradition. His principal theological works are harshly critical of Muslims who do not accept his interpretation of monotheism. The Wahhabis like to refer to themselves as the "true" monotheists. This perspective has led them to destroy tombstones and shrines—even those of the Prophet and his Companions—as the objects of "idolatrous worship" by ordinary Muslims. Ibn Abd al-Wahhab considered such Muslims unbelievers. If they did not realize the error of their ways and failed to respond to reasoning and persuasion (i.e., to Wahhabi proselytization), then, according to Ibn Abd al-Wahhab, such Muslims could be legitimately fought as part of a military jihad.

This Wahhabi ideology—which sharply deviates from mainstream Islamic theology on many critical points—has proved to be influential among a number of radical militant groups of the twentieth and twenty-first centuries in the Muslim-majority world. According to classical Muslim jurists, the military jihad is carried out against non-Muslim enemies. Dissident Muslims who rose up against established governments were treated as political rebels (called in Arabic *bughat*)—not as unbelievers. Their concerns were to be taken seriously by the state and given a fair legal hearing to determine the legitimacy of their political grievances. In contrast, militant groups today are very quick to call other Muslims who disagree with their position "unbelievers." By resorting to this practice of excommunication (*takfir*), such militant groups today resemble the early radical group called the Kharijites, who were known for similarly intolerant views toward other Muslims. (The Kharijites were an extremist minority faction that arose in the middle of the seventh century during the time of the fourth caliph Ali ibn Abi Talib. They regarded other Muslims who did not share their views on specific points of doctrine to be unbelievers who could legitimately be killed. Ali fought them, and they eventually faded away.)

Who are other influential sources for modern militant groups?

Many modern militants are influenced by the views of a twentieth-century Egyptian revolutionary figure by the name of Sayyid Qutb (d. 1966). Qutb was not a religious scholar by training; he studied literature in Cairo and later worked in the Egyptian Ministry of Education. In the late 1940s, he traveled to the United States on a scholarship to study its educational system and lived in Greeley, Colorado, for two years. During his stay he is said to have been repelled by the materialism and loose sexual morals he encountered in American society and was deeply affected by the racism and anti-Arab sentiment he experienced firsthand. Upon his return to Egypt, Qutb joined the Muslim Brotherhood and became a vocal critic of the Egyptian government and its secular policies. Accused of plotting to assassinate the Egyptian president Gamal Abdel Nasser (d. 1970), Qutb was thrown into prison and tortured. This caused him to become radicalized in his thinking. While in prison he wrote two of his best-known revolutionary tracts in which he described his vision of the perfect Islamic society. Qutb borrowed many of his ideas from Abu al-Ala Mawdudi, the influential South Asian political activist of the twentieth century, and from Hasan al-Banna, the Egyptian founder of the Muslim Brotherhood in 1928. Qutb went further than them in developing a revolutionary militant ideology. He was executed in 1966, but his works continue to be studied and disseminated in radical Islamist circles to this day.

Qutb had very definite views on the military jihad. He strongly opposed the idea that, as presented in Islam's foundational sources, the military jihad is defensive. He says derisively that this is the position of "those who have been defeated spiritually and intellectually" by the adverse circumstances confronting Muslims in the postcolonial period. According to Qutb, such people mistakenly believe that they are enhancing the image of Islam by ridding it of what he calls "its program"—which, in his view, is to remove all tyrants and oppressive systems from the face of the earth. This revolutionary "program" is meant to ensure that all humans worship the one God and no other; not by forcing them to do so but by either putting an end to all other "reigning political systems" or subjugating them. As he sees it, the objective of Islam is unchanging—to win over all humanity to the worship of one God; there can be no negotiation or flexibility concerning this fundamental objective. Whoever resists this hegemonic mission of Islam, as conceived by Qutb, must be ruthlessly fought until surrender or death.

For Qutb, this is the purpose of the military jihad—which is combative and offensive—geared toward, as he phrases it, "the liberation of humanity on earth from the worship of [other] humans." Islam, he declares, is not just a belief or creed; it is a public proclamation of the liberation of human beings from the worship of other humans, which it seeks to achieve by putting an end to "human sovereignty or governance" and replacing it with "divine sovereignty." This is realized on earth by the establishment of the law of God and his authority and thus setting people "free" from the "worship" of or "bondage" to other humans.

This language of "liberation" pervades Qutb's book *Signposts along the Way*, lending a messianic tone to the whole work. This tone is heightened by his use of phrases like the "kingdom of God" to be established on earth, which will replace the "kingdom of man." These terms are not part of an Islamic vocabulary; the notion of the "kingdom of God" reminds one of Christian theological discourses. It is known that Qutb used to frequent churches when he lived in the United States, finding at least some measure of commonality with religious Americans. It appears that the language of the sermons he listened to there had seeped into his vocabulary.

As for Qutb's rhetoric on political revolution, it primarily draws its inspiration from Marxist/socialist theories of political empowerment of the era (which in the 1960s would also influence Christian liberation theologies in Latin America). The totalitarian nature of Qutb's "kingdom of God" on earth is without doubt Marxist in flavor, meant to offer an Islamically-tinged alternative to the socialist utopian schemes being advanced during the early part of the twentieth century. Ironically, Qutb's revolutionary language of liberation thus owes much to the secular political discourses of his time.

Qutb also refers to the "vanguard" of the revolution that will usher in the ideal government of his imagination. Such terminology is right out of the playbook of the socialist utopian movements (specifically Leninism) of the early twentieth century that emphasized the role of such a vanguard.

What is the Jahiliyya?

The term "Jahiliyya" in premodern Arabic sources refers to the historical period before the rise of Islam. It refers to an age of ignorance (of the one God and his message through time) and of recklessness characterized by a lack of self-restraint and temperateness. However, Muslims found certain features of the pre-Islamic period praiseworthy—the practice of hospitality, generosity, and other traits characteristic of the traditional Arab that continued to be emphasized in the Islamic period. The eloquent Arabic of pre-Islamic poetry is also much admired by educated Arabs until the present time.

Modern militants use the term "Jahiliyya" in a novel way. For them it is a term of contempt to signify the morally debased condition of modern humankind from which one can be saved only by joining their camp. Syed Qutb promoted this understanding of Jahiliyya through his writings, which became influential in some quarters. This conception of Jahiliyya marks a departure from the usual understanding of this term in the Arabic-Islamic milieu, and one must seek its origins elsewhere. And indeed we find that Qutb found the inspiration for his version of Jahiliyya in the European totalitarian thought of the twentieth century, particularly as espoused by a man called Alexis Carrel. Carrel was a Nobel prize-winning French Catholic biologist and philosopher, who was accused of collaborating with the fascist government in Vichy France. Carrel lamented what he saw as the sinking of Western culture into crude materialism and moral decay that for him constituted a state of barbarism. This was a situation that could only be remedied by the appearance of an enlightened, elite cadre that would guide the Western world back to the path of self-redemption. This conceptualization must have influenced Qutb's understanding of Jahiliyya as a degraded human state. Such an understanding helped fuel his articulation of the concept of an elite revolutionary vanguard that would pave the way toward the renewal and revival of a global Muslim civilization.

How do militant Islamists justify their violent attacks on other Muslims and non-Muslims?

We get a very good sense of the justifications provided by such radical militants when we look at a tract written by an Egyptian admirer of Sayyid Qutb by the name of Muhammad Abd al-Salam Faraj (d. 1982). The work is titled *al-Farida al-ghaiba* (*The Lapsed Duty*); the duty in question is the military jihad. Faraj, an electrician, was one of the militants belonging to the group al-Jihad that assassinated Nasser's successor, Anwar Sadat, after Sadat signed a peace treaty with Israel in 1982. The tract exhorts Muslims to resort to aggressive military jihad because they are besieged by external and internal enemies—non-Muslims and Muslim "apostates" respectively. Faraj heaped scorn on the scholars of his time because, in his opinion, they had encouraged Muslims to abandon this critical duty.

To establish the obligatory nature of the military jihad under such circumstances, Faraj relies on the well-established practice of selectively quoting Quranic verses and hadiths that may be interpreted as urging the faithful to fight continually against those regarded as their unrelenting enemies. These verses and hadiths are cited without any reference to their original historical contexts so that they appear as absolute pronouncements valid for every time and place. Predictably, Quran 9:5 ("Slay the polytheists where you find them") and, in one instance, Quran 2:216 ("Fighting has been prescribed for you even though you may dislike it") are cited by Faraj and understood by him to have abrogated about 114 verses of the Quran that call for forgiveness of and forbearance with one's adversaries. One such conciliatory verse is Quran 2:109 that states, "So forgive and pardon them [in reference to a certain hostile contingent from among the People of the Book] until God makes His judgment apparent."

Faraj notes the opinion of mainstream scholars who had regarded this verse (Quran 2:109) as unabrogated. This verse would impose considerable restrictions on the interpretation of Quran 9:5 as requiring unending warfare against non-Muslims. Faraj, however, proceeds to say that even if one concedes the unabrogated status of Quran 2:109, it does not diminish in any way the duty to carry out the combative jihad. Since he wishes to privilege the understanding of jihad as unending warfare against non-Muslims and "dissident" Muslims, Faraj does not (or cannot) attempt to reconcile the meaning of these two verses. Instead, he cites a hadith in which the Prophet remarks, "Jihad will continue until the Day of Resurrection." This is not an unexpected tactic in militant discourses. Extremists often use hadiths, sometimes of doubtful reliability, to undermine the meaning of a verse, such as Quran 2:109, that is inconvenient for them. Furthermore, jihad as occurs in this hadith is framed as a reference to fighting only, whereas it could be understood to refer more broadly to human struggle on many levels.

Faraj appeals to the fourteenth-century jurist Ibn Taymiyya's pronouncements against the Mongols, which are generalized to all "lapsed" Muslims in his tract. The Mongols were a Central Asian people who attacked the Middle East in the thirteenth century and laid waste to Baghdad in 1258. The Mongol onslaught continued during the thirteenth and early fourteenth centuries when Ibn Taymiyya lived. Faraj speaks approvingly of Ibn Taymiyya's edict in which he condemned the Mongols as "apostates" even after their conversion to Islam. Ibn Taymiyya accused the Mongols of continuing to follow their tribal law instead of Islamic law. In his view, they did not therefore qualify as Muslims and could legitimately be fought. Faraj draws a comparison between the Mongols and the rulers of his time in Muslim-majority societies whom he considers unrighteous. The chilling purpose of this comparison is clear: Faraj and his cohort thereby derive a mandate to justify in their minds the assassination of Egyptian president Anwar Sadat (and potentially other Muslim rulers) deemed to have lapsed from Islam.

Carrying out the military jihad on the extensive scale that these militants have in mind would require state apparatus and a regular army. Accordingly, Faraj stresses the importance of establishing an "Islamic state" and reviving the historical caliphate of the first century of Islam. The Quran makes no reference to any form of government, including the caliphate. To establish its necessity, Faraj cites the one hadith, narrated by the ninth-century scholar Ahmad ibn Hanbal, in which Muhammad predicts that the Rightly Guided caliphate will follow the age of prophethood, after which governance will degenerate into kingship. On the basis of this slim textual evidence, Faraj proceeds to assert what he considers the binding necessity of reviving this idealized caliphate for contemporary Muslims.

A tension now becomes evident in Faraj's thought—if the Islamic state led by the legitimate caliph is necessary to wage this all-out war against the forces of evil, where do Faraj and his supporters derive the mandate to stage their jihad against the unjust majority in the absence of the Islamic state? The answer lies in their appeal to the urgency of the times in which they live—the current situation of Muslims is so dire and desperate, assailed as they are by ungodly enemies (internal and external) who covet their land and assault their dignity, that the combative jihad, they argue, is now an act of self-defense. It is, therefore, no longer a collective duty but an individual obligation. Faraj says fighting the "near enemy" (Arab governments) takes priority over fighting the "far enemy"

(Western governments); thus, "we have to establish the Rule of God's Religion in our own country first." The contingent of God's true warriors, a beleaguered minority in the Islamic world, will eventually establish the "Islamic state," asserts Faraj, and give the lie to those who say that the ideal Muslim community will come about through peaceful propagation of the faith.

Like all extremists, Faraj is dismissive of the view that the internal, spiritual jihad is a higher priority than the physical, combative jihad. He references scholars like Ibn Qayyim al-Jawziyya (d. 1350) who had regarded the hadith that refers to the greater and the lesser jihad as forged. This evaluation is interpreted by Faraj to imply that Ibn Qayyim had rejected the concept of a spiritual jihad.

This is a gross misrepresentation of Ibn Qayyim's views. Ibn Qayyim had a very high regard for the greater internal jihad. He wrote a whole treatise in praise of the spiritual jihad titled (in English translation) *The Preparation of the Patiently Forbearing Ones and Treasures of the Grateful Ones*. In this work, he describes the spiritual jihad as a concept and practice firmly anchored within the Quran and an indispensable part of the human's struggle to flourish spiritually on earth. Whether one hadith referring to this concept was fabricated or not did not lessen its importance for him. For Faraj and his cohort, however, jihad has one predominant meaning—unending violence against all those who refuse to see things their way. Misrepresentation of the views of classical scholars to invent support for their militant views is a well-established tactic for them.

Have Shii thinkers called for political revolution as a form of jihad in the twentieth century?

The most notable Shii revolutionary figure of the twentieth century is Ayatollah Ruhollah Khomenei (d. 1989). Khomeini is best known as the architect of the Islamic Revolution in Iran in 1979. Born in Khomein in southwestern Iran in 1902, he studied in the seminaries in the Iranian city of Qom and launched his own teaching career there, becoming recognized as a prominent jurist and Shii religious authority. Unlike many other Shii jurists of his time, however, Khomeini became active in political affairs and took part in strenuous opposition to several secularizing and Westernizing policies of the Iranian government at the time. The Shah of Iran, a strong ally of the United States, imprisoned Khomeini in 1963 and subsequently had him exiled from Iran. The latter made his way to Turkey and then to Najaf in Iraq, before his triumphant return to Iran from France where he had taken up temporary residence in February 1979. After his return, the monarchy was abolished, and Iran was declared an Islamic republic under the rule of "the guardian jurist" (known in Persian as *vali-ye faqih*).

In the premodern period, most Shii scholars, in contrast to Sunni jurists, had little to say about the military jihad and the rules of warfare. For the largest Shii denomination called the Twelvers who are the majority in Iran and Iraq, the military jihad could no longer be carried out after their rightful Imam disappeared in 874 CE because only he could command a legitimate military campaign.

Khomeini broke out of this mold in the twentieth century by writing a short treatise titled *Jihad al-Nafs aw al-Jihad al-Akbar* (*Spiritual Struggle or the Greater Jihad*) in which he describes the centrality of jihad as continual human striving on earth. Jihad in Khomeini's conceptualization is essentially a social and political struggle against injustice and oppression that ultimately leads to a movement of political liberation. Khomeini addresses his treatise primarily to scholars who are to be the vanguard of the coming revolution against unjust rulers. Such views mirror those of Sunni activists like Mawdudi and Qutb. (Modern Shii and Sunni political activism share much in common as far as objectives and rhetoric are concerned.) According to Khomeini, the revival of religious learning among the scholars and the process of perfecting one's character—the internal struggle—are the necessary preludes to launching a successful external struggle against the impious rulers of contemporary Iran and removing them from power. Through purification of their selves and reform of their conduct, the scholars will be able to overcome all the obstacles placed in their way and undermine every scheme devised to colonize them. Khomeini uses the term "colonization" here not in reference to external Western powers but to the rule of the Shah. When the scholars are able to carry out all their actions for the sake of God and have cleansed their hearts of love for the world, then they will be able to mount an effective resistance against their unscrupulous rulers, he says.

The waging of jihad against such external enemies is not a militant enterprise. Khomeini defines this jihad as a program of nonviolent resistance and withholding cooperation with unjust rulers. Following in the footsteps of the Shii Imams (religious leaders) who had adopted such quietist methods of resistance, Khomeini advocates that "all relations with such rulers be severed and that no one collaborate with them in any way." Illegitimate war, he says, is waged by imperialist governments, such as the Shah's monarchy and the US government, which foster injustice and arrogance in the world. Such wars are opposed to a properly constituted jihad that is waged on behalf of the weak and the oppressed to restore a just sociopolitical order. In this enterprise, Shii scholars, like Qutb's elite vanguard, must lead the way.

What were Usama bin Laden's views on jihad?

When we look at the public statements of Usama bin Laden (d. 2011), the acknowledged mastermind behind the September 11 attacks, we find a declaration of revenge promising unending violence against all those regarded as the enemy in the name of jihad. The enemy is both "imperfect" Muslims and non-Muslims, who have collectively laid siege to the small minority of "true" Muslims whose mission is to save the world. Usama bin Laden and his supporters, as the wronged Muslims, must fight back in self-defense. This defensive jihad, as they see it, has become an individual obligation from which no "true" Muslim is exempt.

When Bin Laden was attending the King Abdulaziz University of Jeddah in the 1970s, he absorbed such ideas from some of his teachers there. One of them was Abdullah Azzam, a Jordanian cleric who had a degree in Islamic jurisprudence from famed al-Azhar University in Cairo. Azzam is sometimes described as the "godfather of global jihad" because of his fiery rhetoric on the necessity of carrying out unrelenting violent attacks to liberate Islamic lands from the rule of non-Muslims and those he regarded as "apostate" Muslims.

Another such champion of militancy was Muhammad Qutb, the brother of Sayyid Qutb. In his classes at King Abdulaziz University, Muhammad Qutb preached the radical views of his brother. Even though he studied business administration, Bin Laden appears to have been profoundly influenced by such radical ideologies. When in 1979 the Soviet Union invaded and occupied Afghanistan, Bin Laden became involved in the armed resistance against the Soviets. In 1982 he traveled to Afghanistan to fight there. This marked the start of his career as a militant who saw violence as the primary means to battle foreign occupation and, particularly, to turn back the tide of non-Muslim infiltration of Muslim territory. By 1990, Bin Laden was at cross-purposes with the Saudi monarchy whose enlistment of American troops to defend the kingdom he severely condemned. He developed an intense hatred of the United States as a country that propped up what he considered to be "un-Islamic" regimes, like the Saudi government, and his name was implicated in a number of terrorist incidents directed at US facilities throughout the 1990s.

According to Bin Laden, the dire circumstances in which jihad is to be carried out by the beleaguered minority of "true Muslims" like himself made permissible all manner of violent action. The accusation of terrorism is meaningless to Bin Laden; this wrong-headed label, as far as he is concerned, is rather to be worn with pride. After September 11, 2001, Bin Laden praised the attack on the United States and claimed credit for it. He proclaimed chillingly:

> And they [the attackers] have done this because of our words—and we have previously incited and roused them to action—in self-defense, defense of our brothers and sons in Palestine, and in order to free our holy sanctuaries. And if inciting for these reasons is terrorism, and if killing those that kill our sons is terrorism, then let history witness that we are terrorists.

"Defensive jihad," in Bin Laden's construction, has degenerated into a vicious spiral of punitive violence, in the carrying out of which he and his followers glory.

What are "martyrdom operations" and when did they start?

The origins of modern so-called martyrdom operations, according to some accounts, may be traced to the actions of a thirteen-year-old Iranian boy, Mohammed Hossein Fahmideh, during the Iran-Iraq War of 1980–1988. In November 1980, Fahmideh is said to have attached rocket-propelled grenades to his chest and blown himself up underneath an Iraqi tank, for which action he was declared a martyr and national hero by Ayatollah Khomeini. The term "martyrdom operations," however, is said to have been coined in spring of 1994, when the militant Palestinian group Hamas carried out suicide attacks in Israel.

How do militant Islamists justify suicide attacks?

Hard-line Islamists and radical ideologues have a range of opinions on the legitimacy of suicide bombings. A number of them acknowledge that such acts constitute suicide and are thus unambiguously prohibited by Islamic doctrine and law. Others come up with clever explanations to get around this prohibition in an attempt to classify them as legitimate, even obligatory, acts of self-defense in specific circumstances.

One such ideologue is Abu Basir al-Tartusi, a Syrian cleric whose views are often cited in discussions of suicide attacks. In one of his electronic publications, he declared that martyrdom operations are indeed closer to suicide than to martyrdom, and thus illicit and forbidden. He cites particularly Quran 4:29 ("Do not kill yourselves, indeed God is merciful toward you") and Quran 2:195 ("Spend in the way of God and do not cast yourselves into destruction with your own hands") to establish the prohibition against taking one's life. He quotes several hadiths that sternly forbid suicide, including the much-cited "Whoever takes his own life with something in this world will be tormented by it on the Day of Resurrection." Abu Basir acknowledges the utter impermissibility of taking innocent human life, Muslim or non-Muslim, according to several Quranic verses (e.g., 4:93, 17:33, 48:25) and hadiths. In view of the hadith "whoever hurts a believer there is no jihad for him," how, Abu Basir asks, can one even begin to justify the intentional killing of such a person when it is not even allowed to cause him any harm? He also notes the hadith that states, "whoever kills someone from among the Protected People [Jews, Christians, and other protected religious communities] will not encounter the fragrance of heaven." He acknowledges that the words of this hadith explicitly protect the lives of non-Muslims. These categorical prohibitions against the murder of innocents established by such clear texts cannot be casually dismissed, he states.

Abu Basir concludes by positioning himself between two diametrically opposed groups. The first group consists of religious scholars who explicitly forbid suicide bombings and declare their perpetrators to have committed suicide and thus deserving of punishment in the next world. The second group declares them to be martyrs and worthy of reward in the next world. He considers both positions to be too absolute and thus weak. Even though he considers martyrdom operations to be closer to suicide and therefore objectionable, he recognizes an exception to the general prohibition against suicide as follows. Should the perpetrator of a suicide attack interpret his actions as a last resort for the greater good after all other means of repelling the aggression of the enemy have been exhausted, then he hopes that the suicide bomber will be deemed a martyr, his sins forgiven, and given his due reward. If, however, the attacker knows of the usual prohibition against suicide and is not convinced that the prohibition has lapsed on account of exceptional emergency circumstances and is riddled with doubts about the permissibility of his actions—but proceeds to carry them out anyway—then such a person has indeed committed suicide and is assured of hellfire. If the suicide bomber's actions destroy the lives of innocent people in addition to his, then he has also committed murder and violated the rights of other human beings, for which there is severe punishment, pronounces Abu Basir.

While Abu Basir's arguments betray a deep moral conflict within him, other ideologues have displayed far less uncertainty on this topic and adopted a more favorable stance toward suicide attacks. One such author is Nawwaf al-Takruri who published an influential tract on martyrdom operations in 1997 that has been reprinted several times since then. Like Abu Basir, al-Takruri is fully aware of the scriptural prohibitions against suicide and the consequent legal and ethical obstacles to justifying martyrdom operations. He lists instead practical and tactical reasons for supporting suicide attacks: They inflict the highest number of casualties on the enemy without exacting a similar loss of life among Muslims; they level the playing field against a militarily superior enemy; and they instill fear and despair in the heart of an otherwise formidable and vicious enemy. With their backs against the wall, a hopelessly outgunned people in extreme circumstances are granted, according to al-Takruri, a moral exception to the standard legal and moral prohibitions against the deliberate taking of one's life.

This line of reasoning was repeated most controversially by the Egyptian cleric Yusuf al-Qaradawi (based at that time in Qatar) in 2002, which generated a flurry of negative publicity in the global media. At that time, al-Qaradawi declared martyrdom operations to be the new defensive weapon of the weak against aggressive tyrannical forces and thus to be regarded as a manifestation of the highest form of jihad. The deliberate taking of one's own life is justified under such circumstances, he claimed, since the vastly superior enemy forces are thereby intimidated and harmed. According to such criteria, suicide attacks against Israelis are legitimate. He claims that the general rules of noncombatant immunity do not apply since Israel is a military society where every man and woman can be called up at any moment to serve in the army. By the same criteria, the terror attacks of September 11 are not justified because they were not carried out in self-defense and they resulted in the deaths of many civilians, including many Muslims.

How does ISIS justify its violent actions as jihad?

Various members of the terror group known as the Islamic State of Iraq and Syria (ISIS, also known under its Arabic acronym Daesh) reduce jihad to violent, punitive acts. According to ISIS ideologues, the military jihad has become a duty to be undertaken to wreak vengeance on all those perceived to be their sworn enemies, Muslim or non-Muslim. This view is strongly evident in a publication authored by Abu Bakr Naji (a pseudonym for an ISIS militant) titled *The Management of Savagery*. In this 400-page manual, the writer exhorts ISIS militants to resort to brutal violence to create "regions of savagery," which will force the inhabitants of such regions to submit to them, who in return will promise to create stability. For Naji, violence is an important and necessary tool to be exercised randomly, unrestrictedly, and, well, savagely, so that their so-called caliphate can be established and expanded.

The fourth issue of the magazine issued by ISIS until recently, called *Dabiq*, is titled "Reflections on the Final Crusade." In this issue, ISIS spokesman Abu Muhammad al-Adnani calls on their supporters to kill unbelievers "in any manner or way possible." He goes on to say, "Kill the unbeliever whether he is civilian or military. . . . Every Muslim should get out of his house, find a crusader, and kill him." For ISIS militants, the military jihad is an unending cosmic holy war against unbelievers, including Muslims so considered. There are no noncombatants among them and no method, however barbaric and inhuman, is off limits. The enemy must not only be physically defeated but also psychologically traumatized in ISIS's orchestration of savagery.

Where are the "moderate" Muslims and why do they not denounce extremism?

They are everywhere. Muslims who are "moderate" in their views are in the mainstream of their societies. "Moderation" in the sense of being "balanced," "temperate," and avoiding extremes in one's behavior and beliefs is a cherished concept for Muslims since it is based on the Quran. Quran 2:143 names Muslims as "a moderate community" (*umma wasat*). This term has been interpreted by scholars to mean that Muslims should always strive for justice since that represents the golden mean of society. A just society is fair, equitable, and balanced, without leaning toward one extreme or another.

The views of mainstream Muslims, however, do not receive wide coverage in the global media, particularly in the

West. As a result, many in the United States and elsewhere are left with the impression that Muslims themselves are not condemning acts of terror carried out in their name. In reality, mainstream Muslims denounce extremism and acts of terrorism all the time.[1]

1. Some of these public statements made by Muslim leaders from various backgrounds can be found at these websites (not an exhaustive list):

"Islamic Statements against Terrorism," http://kurzman.unc.edu/islamic-statements-against-terrorism/
"Muslims against Terrorism," https://web.archive.org/web/20110209123524/http://islamfortoday.com/terrorism.htm,
"Muslim Voices against Extremism and Terrorism," http://theamericanmuslim.org/tam.php/features/articles/muslim_voices_against_extremism_and_terrorism_part_i_fatwas/001220
"Muslims Condemn Terrorist Attacks," http://www.muhajabah.com/otherscondemn.php

6

JIHAD IN THE THOUGHT OF MODERN AND CONTEMPORARY MAINSTREAM SCHOLARS

In contrast to militants, modern mainstream scholars and thinkers approach the concept of jihad in a contextualized and holistic manner. They tend to emphasize the term's different layers of meaning that become apparent in specific situations and historical contexts. They maintain that jihad cannot be reduced to military activity alone, as is often the case. In its basic meaning of struggle or striving, jihad can be and is carried out in many different ways in the lives of human beings. Typically, mainstream scholars acknowledge that armed combat may be, has been, and must continue to be a necessary feature of jihad under specific circumstances, but that it is by no means the only or the most important aspect of this complex term.

The various shades of meaning connected to jihad can be recovered by looking at different sources—the Quran, hadith, theological, and morally edifying literary texts—in addition to the legal texts that are overprivileged in discussions of jihad. Above all, these scholars maintain that one must differentiate between what Muslims understand to be the divinely revealed text of the Quran and texts that record human interpretations—the former is universally authoritative for

Muslims and unchanging while the latter are not. Human interpretations vary greatly and must always be understood in their original sociohistorical contexts. This allows one to critically engage this body of interpretive literature.

How do modern Muslim scholars understand the military jihad?

Modern mainstream Muslim scholars typically insist that one must return to the foundational sources of Islam: the Quran above all and the reliable statements (hadith) of the Prophet Muhammad for a proper understanding of the meanings of jihad in all its aspects—moral, ethical, spiritual, and military. This perspective allows them to adopt a more nuanced and critical attitude toward the premodern legal corpus in which jurists expressed their time- and place-bound interpretations of the military jihad as primarily a state-sponsored activity. They accept the views of the classical jurists when they understand them to be in conformity with Quranic injunctions and established prophetic practice. They critically scrutinize and often reject juridical positions that are understood to deviate from these foundational sources, regarding them as the result of the independent reasoning of the jurists in their specific times and places. The validity of such legal positions does not necessarily continue into the modern period.

What do modern Muslim scholars say about abrogation in the Quran?

The adoption of the principle of textual abrogation (*naskh*) has been criticized by a number of modern Muslim scholars. This principle allowed a number of premodern jurists, as well as Quran commentators, to declare certain Quranic verses abrogated by later revelations. In the case of the military jihad, some premodern jurists invoked the principle of abrogation to develop the theory of offensive military attacks and to legitimize this theory as grounded in scripture. Many modern mainstream scholars oppose the principle of abrogation, especially in discussions of the military jihad. Typically, modern anti-abrogation scholars emphasize that the Quran should be read holistically, that is, as a complete text in which all verses are held to be equally binding. Furthermore, the verses should be read cross-referentially so that their meanings can be understood in relation to one another.

One of the most eloquent opponents of the principle of abrogation was the late nineteenth-century Egyptian scholar and reformer Muhammad Abduh (d. 1905). Abduh rejected the interpretation advanced by some premodern jurists that Quran 9:5 (the so-called sword verse) had abrogated the more numerous verses in the Quran that call for forgiveness and peaceful relations with non-Muslims. Like the late ninth-century exegete al-Tabari, Abduh argues that the historical situation with which the verse is concerned—with its internal reference to the pagan Meccans—means that its applicability is restricted to the time of the Prophet. The command contained in Quran 9:5 applied only to the hostile polytheists of his time who had attacked Muslims. Other verses in the Quran advocating nonviolence and peaceful coexistence cannot be held to have been abrogated since their applicability is general, not particular. Therefore Quran 9:5 has no bearing on the directive contained in, for example, Quran 2:109, which states, **"Pardon and forgive until God brings about His command."** The latter is a general commandment whose applicability is not limited by specific historical circumstances.

Abduh questions those who would regard the injunction contained in Quran 9:5, with its clear reference to Arab polytheists, applicable in any way to non-Arab polytheists or to the People of the Book. He points out that the People of the Book are referred to very differently, as in Quran 5:82, which states, **"You will find that the closest in affection to those who believe are those who say we are Christians."** There are additionally hadiths that call for peaceful relations with various groups of people, such as the one which advises leaving the Ethiopians (as well as Turks) alone, as long as they leave Muslims alone. Abduh notes with regret that jurists tended to read a number of these Quranic verses and hadiths through solely a legal lens. As a result, they missed the fundamental point made throughout the Quran that only those who initiate attacks against Muslims and violate their treaties can be fought. Abduh goes on to point out that the verse immediately following Quran 9:5 offered protection and safe conduct to those among the polytheists who wished to listen to the Quran but who did not in the end embrace Islam. The implication is clear—non-Muslims in general who do not wish Muslims harm and display no aggression toward them are to be left alone and allowed to continue in their ways of life.

Abduh further notes that these verses undermine the arguments put forward by some Western scholars that jihad can be reduced to fighting against non-Muslims to bring about their conversion. Abduh highlights Quran 2:256, which forbids forced religious conversion and other verses that allow fighting against only those who initiate fighting (Quran 9:12–13) and which command Muslims to incline to peace when the enemy inclines to peace (Quran 8:61). Wars fought for material gain and for the shedding of blood, as was common among ancient kings, or for revenge and out of religious hatred, as was the case in the Crusades, or for the purpose of seizing the possessions of the weak and demeaning other human beings, as evident in the European colonial wars of his time, are all forbidden by Islamic law. The only kind of war recognized as legitimate in Islamic thought is the defensive war when proclaimed by the recognized leader of the Muslims in the event of an attack upon Muslim territory, continues Abduh.

Furthermore, he reminds us, Islamic law mandates humane conduct during battle, prohibiting attacks on noncombatants, mutilation of bodies, and destruction of the environment. Chafing under European colonial rule in the late nineteenth century in his native Egypt, Abduh forcefully contrasts these humane injunctions to the exploitative policies of Western colonizers, who, as he describes them, hatch various schemes to establish their tyranny over subject peoples.

Are there Muslim scholars who have challenged the views of Islamist militants?

There are many such scholars. Let us start with the early twentieth-century Egyptian jurist Muhammad Imara (d. 2020), who wrote a detailed refutation of the arguments presented by Muhammad Faraj in his militant tract *The Lapsed Duty*.

In this refutation published in 1982, Imara points out the many mistakes Faraj makes in his citations from the Quran and hadith and in references to juridical opinions. For example, Faraj and his cohort understand certain hadiths that speak of Islam reaching the "East" and the "West" as implying that Islam was intended to be the one and only religion for all humankind. These reports, Imara argues, should not be read this way, because every place has "its east" and "its west"; thus God describes himself as "Lord of the Easts and the Wests." These reports should also be interpreted in light of the Quran itself that contains clear references to multiple communities that follow different religious laws as mandated by God himself. Quran 11:118–119 states, **"If your Lord had willed, he would have made humankind a single community, but they remain diverse, except for those upon whom God has mercy. It is for this purpose that He has created them."** Many commentators have interpreted this verse to mean that God purposefully created this diversity among humans. Imara invites the reader to reflect on the sharp contrast between learned commentary of this sort produced by thoughtful scholars and what he describes as the provocative and baseless speech of Faraj and his followers intended to inflame the passions of youth and pander to the ignorant.

Imara proceeds to a discussion of Quran 9:5 and Faraj's use of it as a verse that abrogates all other verses of forbearance, forgiveness, reconciliation, and gentleness. Imara criticizes

Faraj and his supporters for ignoring that the verse was revealed specifically concerning the polytheists of the seventh century and refers to no other group. To derive a broader and more general applicability of this verse violates the rules of logic and proper understanding of the revelations of God, says Imara. In the rest of the ninth chapter, the Quran unambiguously upholds these fundamental principles: (1) Muslims can resort to armed combat only when the Meccan polytheists (this is the only group referenced in this chapter) start to fight, and (2) military activity is a response to the violation of their pacts with Muslims. Violence, our author affirms, cannot be justified otherwise; the spreading of religion is not sanctioned by the Quran as a reason for beginning hostilities. During the Prophet's time, Muslims took up arms to protect the weak who were persecuted by the Meccan polytheists, as exhorted in Quran 4:75–76:

> What ails you that you do not fight in the path of God while the weak among men, women, and children cry out, "Our Lord, deliver us from this town whose people are oppressors, and grant us from your presence a protector and supporter!" Those who believe fight in the path of God and those who disbelieve fight in the path of the wrongdoers. So fight the allies of Satan; indeed the schemes of Satan are weak.

Imara also criticizes Faraj for calling contemporary Muslim rulers "unbelievers." Faraj alleges that they deserve this name because they commit major sins and they display their lack of faith in public. Imara finds these views alarming and proceeds to refute them. Historically speaking, he says, only the early extremist group Kharijites, to the exclusion of any other faction, has maintained that those who commit major sins have lapsed from the faith. By adopting their dangerous position of declaring other Muslims to be unbelievers, Imara asks, had not the militants themselves become like the Kharijites? Equally troubling is that this accusation of unbelief based on the commission of a major sin could be leveled at anybody, not just a ruler—clearly an act of extremism.

Jihad, Imara reminds the reader, has multiple meanings, challenging those who would assert that it essentially means "fighting" (qital). He says that the term's basic meaning is to exert oneself to the best of one's ability to fend off enemies in different spheres of human life. These enemies range from one's base thoughts to desire for material gain to people who wish you harm. In this broader, holistic sense, "jihad" can refer to struggling against external enemies as well as to combating the lower, animal self and attempting to overcome its incitements to do what is wrong. Different kinds of jihad are thus carried out in different spheres of life.

A more recent critique of militant views was published by the Syrian jurist, public intellectual, and television preacher Muhammad Said Ramadan al-Buti (d. 2013). Al-Buti obtained his doctorate from al-Azhar University in 1965 and served as dean of the Sharia faculty at Damascus University for a while and continued to teach there until his death. In 1993 he published a book titled *al-Jihad fi-l-islam* (*Jihad in Islam*).

Al-Buti begins this important work by directly challenging the prevalent assumption that jihad, which he describes as "a fundamental part of Islamic legal rulings and prescriptions," was commanded only in the Medinan period after the hijra, or emigration, and that it did not exist as a concept and requirement in the Meccan period. Not so, he says. The Meccan phase of the Prophet's career "was filled with jihad," as was the Medinan phase. Because most people tend to define "jihad" in a military sense, and since the combative jihad was permitted only in the Medinan period, this has led to the mistaken assumption that jihad in general was commanded only after the emigration to Medina. This misconception, al-Buti continues, arises from the fact that the multiple meanings of the term "jihad" evident during the Meccan period have been lost. Jihad came to acquire narrower meanings after this period due to specific historical circumstances.

An important component of the jihad of the early Muslims, says al-Buti, was their constant engagement with the Book of God (the Quran) and reflection upon it and their fearless proclamation of the message contained within it, without any regard for the dangers they subsequently faced. These most important forms of jihad were set in motion by Quran 25:52, which specifically refers to this kind of striving with the Quran and its proofs and characterizes it as "a mighty striving" (*jihad kabir*). This characterization indicates its central position among the various forms of jihad. These various forms of striving, which have nothing to do with fighting, constitute the foundation and essence of jihad, al-Buti stresses.

Hadiths, such as the one in which Muhammad says, "The best jihad is a word of truth before a tyrannical ruler" and "the best jihad is your striving against your soul and base desires for the sake of God Almighty," provide further support for these nonmilitary meanings of jihad. Al-Buti invites the reader to reflect on all these proof-texts and realize that this aspect of jihad firmly established in Mecca at the dawn of Islam is the source of the various dimensions it acquired in the following period. The early Meccan noncombative meanings of jihad represent the firmly grounded trunk of a tree that endures under all circumstances, while the military dimension is equivalent to the branches which sprout and die from time to time, according to the needs of varying circumstances. Phrased differently, al-Buti says, the Meccan noncombative jihad is equivalent to basic nutrition that no human can do without under any circumstance, while the military jihad is a medication that one uses to escape from hunger and disease—that is, only under exceptional circumstances.

After the emigration to Medina, the first united Muslim community (*umma*) was established by the Prophet. This society included not only the Meccan Emigrants and the Medinan Helpers (the name given to the Muslims in Medina

who helped their Meccan coreligionists after the emigration in 622) but also the various Jewish tribes of Medina, all
of whom pledged to coexist in peace. This arrangement was
drawn up by Muhammad according to the terms of the document that is called the "Constitution of Medina" in English. Al-
Buti emphasizes that this was the first "Abode of Islam" with
a well-defined territory whose inhabitants—Muslims from
Mecca, Muslims from Medina, and Jews from Medina—were
entrusted with its defense; this was the new dimension of jihad
in Medina.

Buti strongly takes issue with contemporary militants who
argue that Quran 9:5 establishes offensive jihad as a permanent obligation upon Muslims and does not allow Muslims to
coexist peacefully with non-Muslims. He notes that the command to kill the Meccan polytheists in Quran 9:5 was based
on their violent hostility toward Muslims and not on their
unbelief. This was the position of many early scholars. Like
Abduh and Imara before him, al-Buti comments that if Quran
9:5 is understood to command the fighting of polytheists until
their death or their acceptance of Islam, such a command
is overturned by the very next verse (Quran 9:6)that urges
Muslims to offer refuge and safe conduct to polytheists, while
they are in their state of polytheism. He dismisses as irrespon-
sibly arbitrary the view of those who suggest that Quran 9:5
abrogates Quran 9:6, which goes against the usual rule of abrogation that a later verse may override an earlier one.

Al-Buti concludes by summarizing what he calls "the most
important principles of peace and war" in regard to jihad. First
and foremost, he says that "world peace" is the pivot around
which Islamic law and its regulations revolve. The clearest expression of this fundamental principle is found in Quran 2:208,
which states, "**O those who believe, enter into peace [al-silm]
altogether, and do not follow the steps of Satan, for he is an
avowed enemy to you.**" Peace, however, "cannot exist nor
grow except under the reign of justice," he says. Seeking peace
without seeking justice can result in blameworthy submission

to wrongdoing and oppression; "just peace" is never achieved under conditions of continuous violation of the rights of others. This means that Israelis who occupy Palestinian territory and areas in southern Lebanon (note: the latter was true at the time al-Buti wrote his book in 1993) should legitimately be resisted and fought against. Al-Buti stresses that this resistance is not on account of their being Jews but on account of their becoming oppressors. Muhammad had included, for example, the Jewish tribe of Banu Qaynuqa as a full member of the Medinan community (umma) in the Constitution of Medina. The members of this tribe were punished only after evidence of their treachery and hostility became apparent and they clearly posed a danger to Muslims and their allies.

Al-Buti affirms that sincere commitment to peace must necessarily include a sincere commitment to justice. One must strive earnestly to realize just peace. Al-Buti reminds us that according to the Quranic vision, justice is due to all, not just to Muslims.

Are there Muslim scholars who have denounced the views of Usama bin Laden and his followers after the September 11 attacks?

One of the best refutations of the militant positions developed by Usama bin Laden and his followers was written by Ali Juma, the former mufti (chief jurisconsult) of Egypt and professor of Islamic jurisprudence at al-Azhar university in Cairo. It is titled *Jihad in Islam* (like al-Buti's book) and was published in 2005.

Juma begins by highlighting a verse from the Quran (21:107) that addresses Muhammad in the following way: "**We have sent you only as a mercy to the worlds.**" Juma emphasizes that the scope of this verse is vast, embracing every era and every place and applicable to every generation of people, believer and nonbeliever, Arab and non-Arab. The quality of mercy possessed by the Prophet is "general and comprehensive," he says, which colored his temperament and actions toward every living being around him. The point is clear—the fundamental message of Islam is one of mercy, and its spirit must inform everything a Muslim does in imitation of the practices of Muhammad. Such a message is in striking contrast to what militants say and do, especially when they sow fear, terror, and destruction in the name of Islam.

The theoretical basis of jihad, Juma says, is derived primarily from the Quran and the sunna. According to these two sources, "one who strives in the path of God" does so for noble and morally uplifting purposes. Such people are capable of promoting what is good and forbidding what is wrong, for they have internalized the highest virtues and practice them regularly in their lives, avoiding personal ambition or national chauvinism or worldly motivation. Fighting, which is always a time-bound activity, is, therefore, the lesser struggle while the continuous struggle to discipline one's self is the greater one. Although Juma does not anywhere in his short treatise refer explicitly to those who carried out the September 11 attacks or other extremists, his description of a legitimate military jihad clearly runs counter to the tracts of modern-day militants who depict jihad as a never-ending divinely sanctioned battle to avenge past and present wrongs (real and imagined). This is how they justify their refusal to honor traditional restrictions imposed by the jurists on harming noncombatants, destroying property, and so forth.

Juma anticipates a question that may be posed to Muslims today: What is their response to those who point out that most modern nations agree that conflicts are better settled through peaceful arbitration, making wars null and void, whereas "this Quran of yours urges you to undertake the military jihad eagerly?" The answer would be: "We [Muslims] marshal [as our proof-text] in this age the Almighty's words, 'If they should incline to peace, then incline to it also and place your trust in God, for He is the all-hearing and all-knowing'" (Quran 8:61). This verse, Juma says, indicates the eternal wisdom and abiding miracle of the Quran in that it foresaw a future world where global nonviolence was a possibility. Juma suggests that the combative jihad was necessary for self-defense in a pre-modern, war-torn world; against such a historical backdrop, the Quran permitted fighting out of necessity while imposing humane and ethical restrictions on waging war. In the modern world governed (at least theoretically) by international treaties and contracts, Muslims can highlight Quran 8:61 as the appropriate proof-text that mandates peaceful relations among nations.

Are there Muslim scholars speaking out against suicide bombings?

A number of prominent religious scholars and clerics have categorically condemned suicide bombings and declared them unjustified and prohibited. Among such scholars was the well-known Albanian-born scholar of hadith, Muhammad al-Albani (d. 1999), who settled in Egypt. He has been quoted as saying: "Suicide missions at the present time, all of them, are not legislated [by Islam] and all of them are unlawful. They are a form of suicide which causes a person to remain in Hellfire eternally. . . . These suicide missions are absolutely not Islamic."

In 2006, the Saudi scholar Muhammad ibn Salih al-Uthayman, when asked about the legality of suicide attacks, issued a formal legal opinion in which he declared the perpetrator of such attacks to be no different from someone who intentionally takes his own life. This is an act that is categorically prohibited within Islam according to Quran 4:29, which unambiguously states: "**Do not kill yourselves. Surely, God is Most Merciful to you**." Al-Uthayman harshly criticized those who support suicide attacks because "they do not desire anything except revenge against the enemy, by whatever means, be it lawful or unlawful. So they only want to satisfy their thirst for revenge."

A blistering 600-pages long condemnation of suicide bombings was issued by the Pakistani cleric Muhammad Tahir-ul-Qadri in 2010, a summary of which has been translated into English. Among the points forcefully made by Qadri is that "terrorism, in its very essence, is an act that symbolises infidelity and rejection of what Islam stands for. When the forbidden element of suicide is added to it, its severity and gravity becomes even greater." This has been the unanimous position, he asserts, of scholars throughout 1,400 years of Islamic history. Quranic verses and hadiths support this unambiguous prohibition.

Qadri proceeds to elaborate upon the classical laws concerning the humane conduct of warfare that require ensuring the immunity of noncombatants during battle and avoiding the destruction of places of worship, buildings, crops, and trees. Anyone who violates these Islamic conventions of humane warfare cannot claim to be carrying out jihad and "has no relation to Islam and the Holy Prophet," he declares. Qadri deals directly with the argument of militant ideologues that correct intention relieves one of the necessity of adopting correct means in order to realize a just objective.

Not so, he says; in Islamic law, lawful objectives can be attained only through lawful means. For example, constructing a mosque is always a pious act, but one cannot fund its construction by robbing a bank. The good is never served by evil means. The famous hadith, "Actions are judged according to their intentions" is not meant to "set a wrong thing right," rather, it is in reference to "those actions that are proven pious, permissible and lawful." Actions that are unethical, unjust, and unlawful to begin with cannot be rendered their opposite through good intentions alone.

Qadri's extensive critique of suicide terrorism remains one of the most detailed and powerful rebuttals to the violent ideologies crafted by Islamist militants that glorify such activity.

Why don't Muslim scholars collectively denounce terrorism?

Actually they have. On November 9, 2004, King Abdullah of Jordan released a public proclamation in the capital city of Amman that became known as the "Amman Message." The proclamation "sought to declare what Islam is and what it is not, and what actions represent it and what actions do not." Its objective was to explain "the true nature of Islam and the nature of true Islam."

In July 2005, King Abdullah held a follow-up conference in Amman where he convened two hundred of the most prominent Muslim scholars from fifty countries, representing eight recognized schools of law within Islam: Maliki, Hanafi, Hanbali, Shafii (all Sunni), Jafari and Zaydi (Shii), Zahiri (minority legal school), and Ibadi (the latter-day nonviolent incarnation of seventh-century Kharijism). These scholars expressed their consensus on some key issues in the Amman Message. These issues include human rights, individual rights and freedoms, and social justice; the need to condemn and prevent acts of terrorism and aggression, including the carrying out of offensive jihad and murder in the name of religion; the need to guarantee respect and tolerance for other religions, and ensure freedom of religion. The Amman Message also addressed the need for Muslims to be law-abiding, loyal, and good citizens in non-Muslim countries where they are not oppressed or persecuted, enjoy equal justice before the law, and benefit from the freedom to practice their culture and religion. The Amman message may be accessed at Amman Message—The Official Site (https://ammanmessage.com).

The Amman Message remains a bold and timely statement in the modern Muslim-majority world, expressing the firm consensus of the most prominent scholars of the various schools of law that terrorism and unprincipled violence violate the basic teachings of Islam. This scholarly consensus effectively marginalizes those who adopt such tactics in the name of Islam and places them firmly outside the mainstream.

Have Muslim scholars denounced ISIS and its militant views?

Yes, they have indeed. In September 2014, 122 prominent Muslim scholars, jurists, and community leaders came together to prepare and sign a document that contained a stinging denunciation of ISIS and its campaign of militancy. The document was an open letter to Abu Bakr al-Baghdadi, the self-proclaimed "caliph" and leader of ISIS. Known as the "Letter to al-Baghdadi," it presented a detailed theological and legal refutation of the supporters of ISIS. Directly addressing the self-styled caliph, the letter states: "You have misinterpreted Islam into a religion of harshness, brutality, torture and murder. This is a great wrong and an offense to Islam, to Muslims and to the entire world." Above all, the document reminded the self-styled caliph that Islam forbids the killing of innocent civilians, who include ambassadors and diplomats, journalists, and aid workers, among others. Furthermore, the military jihad is defensive, and military activity cannot be undertaken without the right cause, the right purpose, and adherence to the right rules of conduct.

The letter went on to detail specific violations of essential Islamic principles and practices carried out by members of ISIS. It expresses the wide-ranging consensus of prominent Muslim scholars that terrorism as practiced by ISIS is about as far from a legitimate military jihad as one can get. This remains a historic document, which categorically establishes that ISIS is a pariah within the Muslim-majority world and that its members' inhuman acts of violence flout foundational moral and ethical principles within Islamic thought and law.

The "Letter to al-Baghdadi" may be accessed at http://www.lettertobaghdadi.com/14/english-v14.pdf.

What are the main differences between militants and mainstream scholars of Islam today on the issue of violence?

When we compare the perspectives of militant extremists and mainstream Muslim scholars on violence, two glaring discrepancies can be summarized as follows: The first is a matter of reading strategy—militants typically will quote (or misquote) a handful of Quranic verses and hadiths in isolation to justify their violent campaigns, while mainstream scholars insist on a holistic and contextualized reading of these foundational religious texts to define and restrict the boundaries of legitimate military activity. The second concerns the treatment of noncombatants: Militant extremists understand "unbelievers" in general—that is to say, all others (Muslims and non-Muslims) but themselves—to be fair game for attacks and brutalization. This understanding allows them to attack civilians: women, children, and unarmed men who do not fight. In contrast, mainstream scholars are adamant on this point—civilians, regardless of their religious affiliation, cannot ever be targeted; neither can there be wanton destruction of property. Classical jurists declared those who violated this fundamental rule and sowed terror among civilian populations to be carrying out *hiraba*—a legal term that today we may translate as "terrorism." Hiraba is completely outside the boundaries of a legitimate military jihad. This point has been forcefully repeated by modern mainstream Muslim scholars.

Such scholars unfailingly affirm what Qadri asserted: The good is never served by evil means. To establish a just and humane society on earth requires just and humane means to achieve it. According to the most prominent Muslim scholars today, there can be no compromise on this fundamental principle. This consensual position marks the fault line between the overwhelming majority of Muslims and a minority of militant extremists who delight in thumbing their noses at this principle and thereby write themselves out of the mainstream global Muslim community.

7

JIHAD AS NONVIOLENT STRUGGLE AND PEACEMAKING

Modern thinkers and practitioners in different religious traditions have begun to emphasize the notion of nonviolent struggle against social and political injustices to bring about long-term sociopolitical changes. They argue that the prospect of armed conflict in a modern, globally connected world, where various nation-states are in possession of stockpiles of deadly weapons, threatens humankind with extinction. In such circumstances, nonviolent attempts to resolve conflicts and preserve the peace should be the preferred option.

These arguments resonate with a number of thinkers and activists within the Islamic tradition. They typically state that peacemaking is mandated by Islam and that the Quran exhorts Muslims to embrace peace over conflict whenever possible. Muslims may invoke peace even on those who harass them for their beliefs and cause them mental anguish. Quran 25:63 praises **"the servants of the All-Merciful who walk humbly on earth; and when the foolish jeer at them, they reply, 'Peace!'"** This is bolstered by Quran 8:61, the quintessential peace verse, which commands Muslims to accept peaceful overtures even from the most hardened enemy, for the pursuit of peace is a noble end in itself. In the contemporary world—vastly different from the premodern one—one can imagine nonviolent alternatives to conflict resolution at local, national, and global levels. This creates an imperative for Muslims to give priority to jihad as a tool for advancing nonviolent struggle against wrongdoing and against various forms of sociopolitical injustices.

This chapter will discuss the thinking of some of the more prominent Muslim advocates of peace and how they draw from religious texts, as well as lived experience, to make the case for nonviolent struggle and peacemaking as the best expression of jihad in the modern world.

Is there pacifism in Islam?

The concept of peace is a central one in Islamic thought and is woven throughout the basic vocabulary and practices of Islam. The Arabic word *salam* means "peace"; it shares its root with Islam, the name for the religion itself. Embrace of Islam is equated with entering a peaceful state in Quran 2:108 and entering the "realm of peace" (*Dar al-Salam*) in Quran 10:25. *As-salam* is one of the ninety-nine names for God in Arabic that are invoked by pious Muslims. Muslims traditionally greet one another by saying "Peace be on you" (*As-salam alaykum*) to which the response is "And peace be on you" (*Wa-alaykum as-salam*). The hadith literature similarly emphasizes the importance of the concepts of nonviolence, peace, and cordiality in relation to the daily life of the pious Muslim. In a report recorded by al-Bukhari, Muhammad commands Muslims to "spread peace among the people." The prevalent attitude among Muslim thinkers is that the divinely revealed ethical principles and laws contained in the Sharia, when properly interpreted and applied, will ultimately lead to the desired goal: a just and peaceful social order.

While peace, peaceableness, and peacemaking are central concepts in Islam, the religion cannot be described as pacifist in its fundamental orientation. Pacifism in its absolute sense is generally understood to mean an unconditional avoidance of violence under any and every circumstance. In general, the Islamic moral landscape is not receptive to the idea of pursuing nonviolence as an ideological end in itself, divorced from the requirement of fulfilling the conditions of social and political justice. Nonviolence, after all, can be (and has been) forcibly imposed by the strong on the weak in violation of the latter's rights and dignity. Pacifism, when defined as nonviolence under all circumstances and the unconditional rejection of armed combat, even in the face of violent aggression, would be regarded in specific situations as facilitating injustice and contributing to social instability. Such a situation would be morally and ethically unacceptable.

The relatively newly coined word "pacificism," on the other hand, better describes traditional Islamic attitudes toward peacemaking. Pacificism refers to a preference for peaceful conditions over war but accepts that armed combat for defensive purposes may, on occasion, be necessary to advance the cause of peace. Conditional pacifism may be another way of referring to this position. In contrast, absolute pacifism harbors the possibility of submitting to injustice and wrongdoing to avoid violence at all costs, a moral scenario that cannot be defended within the Islamic ethos.

Can jihad be understood as nonviolent struggle and peacemaking?

The fundamental moral and ethical imperative within Islam is to uphold and promote what is good and prevent what is wrong. One must resist wrongdoing, even if only verbally or silently in one's heart; refusal to do so represents a grave moral failure on the part of the individual. Communities are similarly charged with carrying out this moral and ethical rule. Peace does not evolve on its own; the establishment of a nonviolent social and world order requires conscious effort and constant vigilance, in addition to peaceful intent. The maintenance of peace requires that those who would seek to undermine it must be resisted through a variety of peaceful means at first and ultimately through principled violence when peaceful means are exhausted. In Islamic thought, jihad refers to this constant human struggle to promote what is essentially right and good and prevent what is evil and wrong in all spheres of life.

A number of modern and contemporary scholars and activists in Muslim-majority and Muslim-minority contexts have focused on the peaceful social activism they understand to be the predominant meaning of jihad. They typically emphasize the practice of patient forbearance (sabr) as the most important aspect of jihad, which allows for enduring nonviolent resistance to wrongdoing. This kind of peaceful resistance may be carried out at the personal, communal, state, and, increasingly today, the global level.

Which Muslim thinkers understand jihad as nonviolent struggle?

This position has been advocated by a number of well-known and less well-known figures. One of the more prominent figures from the early twentieth century is the Pashtun leader Syed Abd al-Ghaffar Khan (d. 1988), also known as Badshah Khan, from the Northwest Frontier Province in current day Pakistan. In the early twentieth century, he organized a peaceful resistance movement called the Khudai Khidmatgars (Servants of God) against the British colonizers of India, who had mounted a brutal military campaign against the Pashtuns. Khan argued that Muslims should adopt nonviolence against oppression on the basis of foundational Quranic principles, especially sabr, exemplified in the life of the Prophet and his Companions.

Similar arguments were made by two of Abd al-Ghaffar Khan's contemporaries: the Syrian scholar and activist Jawdat Said, and the Indian Muslim thinker and prolific writer Maulana Wahiduddin Khan, who passed away in 2021. Their contemporaries in Turkey included Said Nursi (d. 1960), whose teachings continue to be followed by the contemporary

Turkish author and social reformer Fethullah Gulen and his network of supporters.

New cohorts of contemporary Muslim peace scholars and activists are following in the footsteps of these trailblazers. Notable among them is Muhammad Abu-Nimer who is a professor of conflict resolution at American University in Washington, DC. He also directs the Salam Institute there, a nonprofit organization devoted to "research, education, and practice on issues related to conflict resolution, nonviolence, and development with a focus on bridging differences between Muslim and non-Muslim communities." Abu-Nimer similarly emphasizes the cultivation of the Quranic trait of sabr, among other virtues, as an antidote to unprincipled violence. One of his colleagues is Ayse Kadayifci-Orellana; she also teaches conflict resolution at American University and is a founding member of the Salam Institute.

Another prominent scholar-practitioner in the field of Islamic peacebuilding is Qamarul Huda, formerly of the United States Institute of Peace in Washington, DC, who has written on Islamic peacebuilding The Moroccan-born peace activist Houda Abadi runs an organization called Transformative Peace in the United States that specializes in inclusive peace processes, with a focus on women, peace, and security. Ramin Jahanbegloo, a Canadian scholar of Iranian descent, is greatly influenced by Gandhian principles of nonviolence and follows in the footsteps of Abdul Ghaffar Khan and the Indian Muslim intellectual Mawlana Abul Kalam Azad in advocating nonviolence within an Islamic milieu. In Thailand, Chaiwat Satha-Anand (Qader Muheideen), a university professor, has long been an influential voice in the fields of nonviolence and peace studies. These names are some of the best-known ones among Muslim scholar-activists who have embraced nonviolence as the best way to realize the moral imperative of promoting what is good and just on earth and combatting injustice and wrongdoing.

What caused the modern turn toward thinking of jihad as nonviolent struggle?

Starting in the nineteenth century, European colonial occupation of a broad swath of the Muslim world provided the impetus in a number of cases for the rise of nonviolent resistance movements against foreign occupation. Although defensive military jihad also enjoyed a revival, at least at the level of rhetoric, there was an awareness that localized military resistance against a more militarily powerful enemy would prove futile.

Already in the early twentieth century, we find the prominent voice of Abdul Ghaffar Khan, who attained legendary status for his principled nonviolent opposition to British occupation of his homeland. Khan was ethnically a Pashtun from Utmanzai in the Northwest Frontier Province of what is today Pakistan. He was born in 1890 when the Indian subcontinent was under British colonial rule. As part of its brutal policy of repression against the local inhabitants, the British would frequently send armed expeditions to the Northwest Frontier Province to attempt to "pacify" it—beating, jailing, and killing Pashtuns to achieve their goals. The Pashtuns, fabled for their martial prowess, fought back resolutely and frequently repelled the British invaders successfully. They maintained their armed resistance to the foreign occupiers for more than eighty years.

Abdul Ghaffar Khan grew up in this environment and developed a strong inclination to improve the conditions of his people through education and social reform. This desire was nurtured by his Muslim religious upbringing and by what he felt from a young age was a personal call to serve God. In 1910 he established the first non-British school in his region and embarked on a campaign to establish more schools for both males and females. He launched a campaign to dig wells and latrines for the common people and improve their hygiene. Social reform led to a desire to bring about political reform as well; the goal was to achieve self-governance for the Pashtuns.

This was of course a highly risky venture under colonial occupation. Khan faced imprisonment and degrading treatment at the hands of the British as a result of his social and political activism. Undaunted, in 1929, he established a group that he named Khudai Khidmatgars—meaning "Servants of God"—that would resist British occupation and seek to liberate the Pashtuns through completely nonviolent means. Membership in the Khudai Khidmatgars was open to both men and women and to Hindus and Sikhs, in addition to Muslims.

Despite being repeatedly harassed, intimidated, and jailed by the British, Khan persisted in his nonviolent movement and became an ally of Mahatma Gandhi, the better-known Hindu peace activist. Khan's "army of peace" continued to attract recruits until the end of British rule in 1947. He died in an independent Pakistan, where he faced resistance to his ideas. In recent years, Khan's thought and movement have attracted the attention of some international proponents of nonviolent activism, who take heart from the example he set in very challenging circumstances.

A younger contemporary of Abdul Ghaffar Khan was the Indian Muslim scholar and activist Wahiduddin Khan (no relation), who was born in 1925 and recently passed away on April 21, 2021. Like Abdul Ghaffar Khan, Wahiduddin Khan was born under the British occupation of his homeland. A number of his family members were engaged in the independence struggle against the British. The campaign against political oppression and social injustice had a profound influence on him and provided the impetus for his religious and social activism. When Abul Alaa Mawdudi in 1941 established the political party called Jamaat-i Islami (The Islamic Association) in India, Khan became a member of it. Khan, however, would break with Mawdudi after fifteen years because of fundamental disagreements concerning the relation between Islam and politics. Unlike Mawdudi, Khan emphasized that belief in monotheism and peaceful submission to God were at the heart of all things Islamic. Political and economic reform was at best a secondary consideration and not the primary motivation for one's commitment to Islam. In 1970 Khan established the Islamic Centre in New Delhi, which has published over two hundred of his books, a number of which have been translated from the original Urdu into English, Arabic, and other languages.

Wahiduddin Khan drew his inspiration for nonviolence from the various stages of Muhammad's prophetic career. Examples he drew from Muhammad's life in support of his nonviolent project include the following: (1) In the Meccan period, the Prophet was primarily concerned with challenging polytheism through peaceful, verbal means; (2) During the thirteen-year Meccan period, the Quraysh became his archenemies, and prominent members of the tribe conspired to kill him, but he avoided physical confrontation and resorted instead to emigration to Medina; (3) The "battle" of the Trench (also called Battle of Khandaq), in which no fighting actually occurred, is a stellar example of avoiding unnecessary violence; (4) As is the Treaty of al-Hudaybiyya that Muhammad signed with the pagan Meccans in 628 to avoid bloodshed; and (5) The peaceful conquest of Mecca in 630 at a time when the Muslims were militarily strong demonstrates the preference for nonviolent methods over violent ones to promote truth and justice. Khan taught his followers that nonviolence was the "weapon of the Prophet" and that it characterized the greater part of his prophetic career before he received divine revelations to defend his community militarily. Khan stressed that he understood the Islamic way of life to consist of deeds, faith, and love.

Is there a theological basis in Islam for promoting peace?

All peace advocates stress the Quranic principle of sabr—as mentioned, a word that can be variously translated as patience, forbearance, endurance, and perseverance. Furthermore, they draw inspiration from verses in the Quran that stress forgiveness and reconciliation and that point to the spiritual and intellectual aspects of jihad.

In his writings, Wahiduddin Khan emphasized Quranic verses such as 42:39, which states: "**He who forgives and is reconciled, his reward is with God.**" He proceeds to establish the peaceful essence of jihad by citing several additional Quranic verses as proof-texts in support of this position; among them Quran 25:52 ("**Do not yield to the unbelievers, but fight them strenuously with it** [i.e., with the Quran]"). Khan stresses that "fighting" with the Quran here implies a spiritual, verbal, and intellectual struggle to overcome falsehood peacefully through the propagation of truth. He also points to Quran 22:78 that exhorts the believer to "**strive** [*jahidu*] **in regard to God a true striving as is His due.**" The Arabic command "jahidu" used in the verse points to this earnest nonviolent struggle for the sake of God, a term, he says, that eventually came to be applied to the early battles in Islam since they were part of this overall struggle.

With regard to the hadith literature, Khan takes special note of a hadith narrated by Aisha, the Prophet's wife, recorded in the highly regarded hadith collection by al-Bukhari. The hadith quotes Muhammad as expressing a preference for the easier of any two options when available in regard to an action. Since war is a hardship, Khan infers from this hadith that the peaceful struggle for truth, which is the easier option for humanity, should be considered superior. On the basis of another hadith found in the well-known collection of the ninth-century scholar Ahmad ibn Hanbal (d. 855), Khan identifies the *mujahid* (one who carries out jihad) in the following ways: as "one who struggles with himself for the sake of God"; "one who exerts himself for the cause of God"; and "one who struggles with his self in submission to the will of God." Jihad is, therefore, essentially a peaceful struggle against one's ego and against wrongdoing in general, he concludes.

Another well-known contemporary peace activist is the Syrian author and intellectual Jawdat Said (b. 1931), who

studied at al-Azhar University in Cairo and obtained a degree
in the Arabic language there. Having experienced the Second
World War and cataclysmic political events in the Middle East
during the colonial and postcolonial periods, he seems to have
turned to nonviolence after a stint in the Syrian military. He
wrote prolifically on the topic of nonviolence despite imprisonment and censure by the Syrian government. He continues
today to live quietly in his ancestral family house in Bir Ajam
in the Golan Heights in Syria.

Said grounds his nonviolent understanding of jihad in his
reading of the Quran, particularly the story of Adam's two
sons, as recounted in Quran 5:27–31. These verses give an
account of the violent altercation between Adam's two sons.
(Unlike the biblical version that refers to them as Cain and
Abel, the two sons are not named in the Quran. Their Arabized
names, Qabil and Habil, occur in the commentary literature.)
The Quranic verses state:

> And recite to them the story of Adam's two sons, in
> truth, when they both offered a sacrifice [to God],
> and it was accepted from one of them but was not ac-
> cepted from the other. Said [the latter], "I will surely
> kill you." Said [the former], "Indeed, God only accepts
> from those who are righteous [who fear Him]. If you
> should raise your hand against me to kill me –I shall
> not raise my hand against you to kill you. Indeed, I fear
> God, Lord of the worlds. Indeed, I want you to obtain
> [thereby] my sin and your sin, so you will be among the
> companions of the Fire. And that is the recompense of
> wrongdoers." And his soul permitted him to murder his
> brother, so he killed him and became among the losers.
> Then God sent a crow searching [i.e., scratching] in the
> ground to show him how to hide the private parts of
> his brother's body. He said, "O woe to me! Have I failed
> to be like this crow and hide the private parts of my

**brother's body?" And he became one of those stricken
by remorse.** (Translation taken from Said's book *Non-Violence: The Basis of Settling Disputes in Islam*)

Among the relevant ethical and moral imperatives that Said
derives from these verses are these three: (a) Muslims should
not call for murder, assassination, or any kind of provocative acts that may lead to the commission of such crimes;
(b) Muslims should not impose their opinions on others by
force or yield to others out of fear of force; (c) Muslims in their
pursuit to spread the word of God "must not diverge from the
true path which was set forth by the prophets from beginning
to end." The third imperative indicates Said's understanding
of jihad as an essentially nonviolent enterprise undertaken by
Muslims for the purpose of bearing witness to the truth and
justice of their faith and to peacefully invite others to listen to
the message of Islam.

Muslims, continues Said, are entrusted with speaking "the
words of truth under any condition." He refers to the hadith
in which Muhammad affirms that the best jihad is speaking a
word of truth to a tyrannical ruler. Said further states that while
bearing witness to truth in this manner, a Muslim may not resort to violence, even apparently in self-defense. He refers to
the hadith in which a Companion asked the Prophet what he
should do if someone enters his house and "stretches his hand
to kill me?" The answer: "Be like Adam's [first] son," and then
Muhammad recited Quran 5:27–31. (Adam's first son was the
one who refused to resist the second son when he threatened
violence against the former.)

Do Muslim peace activists reject the military jihad?

Broadly speaking, Muslim peace practitioners do not reject the
military jihad but consider fighting to be a secondary aspect of
jihad that comes into play in very limited, specific conditions.

Thus, Jawdat Said does not say that fighting is always categorically prohibited; he recognizes jihad "as an ongoing process on condition that a Muslim must know exactly when to resort to armed struggle." "Executing laws," he says, "and carrying out Jihad must only be done by individuals who are qualified for such an important task." The improper and excessive recourse to armed combat in the name of jihad and cynical manipulation of it by unscrupulous people have "caused more harm to Muslims than any other malpractice," he says. Muslims are primarily charged today with preaching the message of God and reforming humans, which can never be accomplished by force. This is clearly stated in the verse "**Let there be no compulsion in religion**" (Quran 2:256).

Said does not deny the existence of verses that command Muslims to fight; he argues that their commands, however, are not applicable in the absence of a properly formed Islamic community, which is the situation in which Muslims now live. A properly formed Islamic community is one where truth and justice reign, inhabited by Muslims "who call for the construction of the Islamic society, its reformation or protecting it against the elements of corruption." They are furthermore those

who have enough courage to declare their creed and everything they believe in, and who are openly denouncing what they believe to be wrong in a clear way. . . . They are the kind of people who, for their cause, persevere patiently with the oppression of others when they are subjected to torture and persecution.

Such patient, nonviolent activism in the face of oppression and injustice and in the absence of the properly constituted Islamic community is the only form of jihad that can be carried out by Muslims today, asserts Said. Adoption of such nonviolent struggle is to follow in the footsteps of all the prophets mentioned in the Quran who patiently endured the harm visited upon them by their own people on account of their preaching the truth. One of the examples Said highlights is that of Moses arguing calmly and peacefully before the Pharaoh in defense of the truth that he had been called to preach. In contrast, says Said, the Pharaoh resorted to aggression, as tyrannical rulers are apt to do, to protect their political dominion. Believers should not resort to the violent overthrow of despotic governments, he counsels, for by adopting violent methods they would be following in the footsteps of the Pharaoh. Like Moses and all the other prophets, they should attempt instead to bring about a peaceful resolution of conflict through the clear and fearless proclamation of the truth.

Similarly, Wahiduddin Khan stresses that the main purpose of Islam in its earliest days was the peaceful propagation of the faith and the spiritual reformation of people; political and social reforms were secondary concerns. He states that Muslim adoption of the principle of nonviolence today recognizes that interpretations of religious commands can change as historical circumstances change. In the premodern period, war was a way of life; now we are able to imagine and implement peaceful strategies for conflict resolution. Khan scoffs at the so-called jihad movements of the contemporary period for their glorification of violence; in these changed circumstances, "launching out on a violent course of action is not only unnecessary, but also un-Islamic." He says derisively that a movement cannot be deemed a jihad "just because its leaders describe it as such." A properly constituted jihad must fulfill the essential conditions decreed by Islamic law. The combative jihad, which is essentially *qital* (armed combat), is an activity undertaken by the state and cannot be placed in the same category as acts of worship, such as prayer and fasting. There is no room, he insists, for nonstate warfare; war, and it must be defensive war, may be declared only by the ruling government. Noncombatants may never be targeted. On this basis, Khan sternly condemns the perpetrators of the September 11 attacks. He also denounces suicide bombings, which he declares to be a complete departure from Islamic norms and practices. Khan comments, "According to Islam we can become martyrs, but we cannot court a martyr's death deliberately." He reminds us that **"God calls to the Home of Peace"** (Quran 10:25) and that this is the best way to realize God's will.

8

JIHAD AND ITS PERCEPTIONS
IN THE WEST

Harvard senior Zayed Yasin, an American Muslim, was invited by a special committee to deliver an address during the university's 2002 commencement ceremony. Yasin accepted and titled his speech "My American Jihad," which was announced to the public. No one was prepared for the uproar that followed the announcement. Some students at Harvard voiced outrage over the word "jihad," which was associated in their minds with violent religious militancy. Yasin responded that he was using the word in its general meaning of a moral and spiritual struggle and had not intended to cause any controversy. He had his share of supporters: The administration backed his right to carry on as planned, as did some students. Some major US newspapers considered the event worthy of note and published breathless accounts of the kerfuffle. A last-minute compromise was reached: The title was dropped from the program, and Yasin delivered his original, prepared speech on commencement day. The *Harvard Crimson*, the university's student newspaper, reported the next day that Yasin's speech was warmly received. With the title removed, the speech appeared little different from a traditional, inspirational commencement address. Yasin had wished to protest the annexation of the term "jihad" by religious extremists to describe their violent deeds, but his detractors could not see beyond the widespread "newspaper" usage of the word.

This incident highlights the sharp disconnect between the way most Muslims continue to understand jihad today and the way many non-Muslim Westerners reflexively react to the word. Some Muslims may stress that they use the term "jihad" in a highly personal way to describe their struggle to achieve academic and professional fulfillment in their lives. Others may use it to describe their activism to address certain kinds of social and political injustices—some Muslim feminists, for example, describe their struggle against gender inequality as a jihad.

These personalized meanings were brought into sharp relief in Chicago in 2013. In that year, Ahmed Rehab, the executive director of the Council on American-Islamic Relations (CAIR) there, started a project called MyJihad to document what the word means to ordinary American Muslims. He took out advertisements that ran on Chicago buses which explained jihad in different ways: one cited the struggle of a Muslim Chicagoan to lose weight; another referred to an Iraqi refugee's effort to start a new life in America as a single mother; while a third described the struggle waged by some Muslim children against bullying classmates.

The 2002 Harvard commencement flap is a somber reminder that jihad had entered Western vocabularies already in the medieval period as a violent military term. This was due to the sometimes bloody conflicts between the worlds of Christianity and Islam in the premodern period as well as in the modern colonial period. Conflicts have continued through the postcolonial period from the first half of the twentieth century until the present time. Jihad is usually imagined by Westerners as the Islamic counterpart of "crusade" and therefore (mis)translated as "holy war." This meaning has solidified in the post-September 11 period. Literature and rhetoric produced by contemporary militant groups in and from Muslim-majority societies tend to underscore this meaning. Western media that gives prominent coverage to the violent acts carried out by Islamist militant groups continue to reinforce these perceptions.

Is there a Western equivalent of the military jihad?

The Western Christian concept of "just war" (in Latin *bellum justum*) comes closest to the Islamic concept of the military jihad, with some differences. Augustine, the fifth-century bishop of Hippo (d. 430), is credited with being the first to formulate a Christian conception of just war, in which he was influenced by the work of the Roman statesman Cicero (d. 43 BCE). Augustine maintained that a just war could be launched to avenge a real injury perpetrated by an external enemy and that it must be proclaimed by the legitimate authority who alone determines the justness of the cause. As for just conduct during warfare, he allowed the killing of noncombatants if that was necessary. In the twelfth century, the Italian Catholic priest and philosopher Thomas Aquinas (d. 1274) would build on Augustine's ideas. Aquinas defined just war as one that met the following conditions: (1) It was fought under the right authority; (2) had a just cause; and (3) was undertaken with right intention. He made no distinction between defensive and offensive wars, and, like Augustine before him, was not concerned with the protection of civilians during war.

Concern for establishing the rules of just conduct during hostilities (in Latin *jus in bello*) would arise much later. Such rules were articulated in the writings of the seventeenth-century Dutch jurist Hugo Grotius (d. 1645), who is regarded in the West as the founder of modern international law. *Jus in bello* considerations require just war adherents to respect the principles of proportionality and discrimination; the latter principle protects the rights of noncombatants during warfare. Grotius incorporated these principles of just conduct in his work the *Law of War and Peace* (in Latin *De Jure Belli ac Pacis*), which provided the basis for a modern law of nations in the West.

Is there an Islamic influence on the development of modern international law?

The additional regulations in Western international law for the protection of civilians do bear a striking resemblance to the Islamic requirements for just conduct in the waging of war. These similarities strongly suggest that these classical Islamic regulations during armed combat, already well established in the early centuries of Islam, influenced the development of *jus in bello* requirements in the modern Western law of nations. It is significant that three jurists whose thought influenced Grotius were from Spain, considerable parts of which had until the fifteenth century been under Muslim rule. In the medieval period, Islamic law was taught in Spain as well as in southern Italy, which were culturally within the Islamic orbit. These three Spanish jurists were Francisco de Vitoria in the sixteenth century and Bartolome de Las Casas and Francisco Suarez in the seventeenth century. They were part of the influential School of Salamanca in Spain that made major contributions to the development of international law in Europe.

In his legal work, Vitoria explicitly identified those who should be considered noncombatants and given protection during military combat: women and children, agricultural laborers, travelers, and the civilian population in general. Las Casas similarly emphasized the need to protect women and children, religious functionaries, serfs, and other noncombatants during war. The requirement that these categories of noncombatants should be protected during armed combat was already well entrenched within the Islamic law of nations or international law (known as *siyar* in Arabic) by the eighth century. The legal philosophy of Suarez, the third jurist, also emphasized that there must be humane rules to order relations with other communities and external polities.

These legal stipulations mirror foundational principles within the Islamic ethical and legal tradition that were already articulated in the writings of the eighth-century jurist Muhammad al-Shaybani (d. 805), who is regarded as the founder of the Islamic law of nations. After al-Shaybani, generations of Muslim jurists would expand on these principles and continue to uphold the requirements of just conduct during military campaigns, with a particular focus on the protection of civilians from harm.

Grotius himself refers fleetingly to Islamic law in his works, but it was not customary in his period to cite one's sources, as it is now for responsible academics. In Western discussions of jus in bello, the Spanish contributions to the development of this concept is readily acknowledged; its probable earlier Islamic genealogy has, however, only occasionally been suggested. The topic of Islamic influence on the development of certain aspects of modern international law is/will be fiercely resisted by those who are ideologically and emotionally opposed to the very idea. Nevertheless, it invites further academic research and inquiry.

Is classical Islamic international law compatible with modern international law?

A number of prominent modern Muslim jurists, who work from a comparative perspective, have highlighted the compatibility of classical Islamic international law with modern international law on key issues concerning war and peace among nations.

The well-known Syrian jurist Wahba al-Zuhayli (d. 2015), for example, identified three specific types of legitimate war in the Islamic context: (1) War against those who prevent the preaching of Islam or against those who create internal disorder and strife; (2) War in defense of individuals and communities who are persecuted; and (3) War to repel a physical attack against one's country. Al-Zuhayli points out that types 2 and 3 are fully compatible with principles of modern international law that allow for self-defense against prior aggression and humanitarian intervention in conflict-ridden regions. These principles governing legitimate warfare within the Islamic legal tradition have parallels in Article 51, which refers to the principle of self-defense and in Chapter VII of the United Nations Charter, which has been recently interpreted by some to potentially allow for humanitarian intervention. Type 1, however, has no clear parallel in international law since it is more of a moral instrument to ensure religious freedom and contain social instability in general.

Like many premodern scholars and jurists, al-Zuhayli underscores that, among its many humanitarian provisions, Islamic law stipulates that noncombatants must not be targeted or harmed during a war. Wanton destruction of property, killing livestock, and laying waste to towns and villages are also prohibited. Humanitarian treatment of prisoners of war is required, and mutilation of corpses is strictly forbidden. Such just rules of conduct during warfare were incorporated late into modern international law. They are included in the 1949 Geneva Conventions and their 1977 Additional Protocols, which form the core of international humanitarian law, as well as in the Nuremberg Charter of 1945, which deals with war crimes.

At the same time, modern scholars of Islamic law have been highly critical of certain rulings within classical siyar. The idea espoused by a number of premodern Muslim jurists that the Muslim ruler can wage preemptive, offensive military campaigns against non-Muslim polities is rejected by modern mainstream Muslim jurists. There is more or less a legal consensus today that Muslims are required to be peaceful toward those who are peaceful toward them and only fight those who fight them. This represents a significant departure from the classical juridical view that the Muslim ruler was obligated to carry out a military expedition once a year as expansionist jihad to expand the boundaries of Islamic territories. Mainstream Muslim jurists today reject this view as insupportable for three reasons. First, it violates the Quran's prohibition against fighting except in self-defense. Second, this ruling was the result of a legal accommodation to a premodern world characterized by non-Muslim hostility to Muslims. Third, war was assumed to be the default situation between nations in the premodern period. There is, therefore, a great need to revisit the classical Islamic rules of war and peace in a vastly altered world in which mutually binding international treaties exist to promote peaceful relations among nations. As many now argue, this revisitation is called for in a spirit of greater faithfulness to Quranic ethics of war and peacemaking.

Are there modern Muslim critics of the concepts of the Abodes of War and Peace?

This binary division of the world had already become quite obsolete by the twelfth century because such a division did not map onto the political realities of the time. Muslim rulers often forged alliances with non-Muslim rulers against a common enemy. There was a constant exchange of merchants, diplomats, and other kinds of visitors between Muslim and non-Muslim lands. Three prominent Egyptian scholars from between the late nineteenth century to the mid-twentieth century—Muhammad Abduh, Rashid Rida, and Mahmud Shaltut—characterized these designations as defunct in the modern period and urged for international relations to be based on mutual respect and peaceful coexistence.

A more recent critic of these concepts was another Egyptian thinker and prolific author Jamal al-Banna (d. 2013), who, unlike his older brother Hasan al-Banna, was known for his socially liberal views. In his 1984 refutation of *The Lapsed Duty* by Abd al-Salam Faraj, al-Banna tackled the concept of Dar al-Harb, or the "House of War." This abode, he says, is composed of nations that are hostile to Islam, aggress Muslims, and violently prevent the propagation of Islam. Under such circumstances, Muslims have the right to retaliate and defend themselves. Non-Muslim nations that neither initiate hostilities against Muslims nor prevent the peaceful dissemination of

Islam may not be fought against; instead, Muslims are required to establish friendly relations with them. Quran 5:51, which counsels Muslims not to take the People of the Book as "allies" (*awliya*), must be understood in this historical vein. Extremist Muslims, as well as anti-Islam Western polemicists, like to cite this verse as a general prohibition against forging peaceful and fraternal relationships with non-Muslims. Al-Banna argues against this interpretation and says the verse only referred to those Jews and Christians who had conspired against Muslims and intended them harm in the seventh century. A blanket denunciation of the People of the Book does not make sense, he continues, in view of the fact that the Quran allows Muslim men to marry Jewish and Christian women and live with them in harmony. These opposing viewpoints constitute a fundamental difference between what al-Banna depicts as the supremacist, violent manifesto of the extremists and the historically-contextualized and scripturally-based arguments of mainstream scholars like himself.

Another modern Egyptian scholar of Islamic international law, Mohammad Talaat al-Ghunaimi, has similarly criticized the concept of the Abode of Islam pitted against the Abode of War as being hopelessly obsolete in the modern world. He recognized the utility of this model during the Abbasid period (from after the mid-eighth century) when, from a medieval realist perspective, such a division of the world made practical sense. In the premodern era, those who were not from one's own world (and particularly from one's own religious community) could reasonably be assumed to be foes rather than friends. States had to remain militarily vigilant against potential aggression from other states that did not share their religious and political allegiances. In our vastly altered historical circumstances, such a bipolar vision can no longer be deemed valid.

It is also argued that Muslim-majority states are now members of the United Nations and are signatories to various international treaties that govern relations between themselves and other nation-states, regardless of religious commitments. The Organization of Islamic Cooperation (OIC), which has fifty-seven members, out of which forty-nine are Muslim-majority countries, explicitly states in its Charter that member nations will conduct relations with other states on the basis of equality and reciprocity. The relevant clause in the OIC Charter states, "We the Member States of the Organization of the Islamic Conference, are determined to . . . uphold the objectives and principles of the present Charter, the Charter of the United Nations and international law as well as international humanitarian law."

The strong points of agreement between Islamic and Western international law outlined here allow both to coexist as parallel and complementary legal systems. Their overlap on significant features facilitates the productive exchange of ideas between Muslim and non-Muslim jurists.

How does the Western media portray jihad?

"Jihad" is more often than not translated as "holy war" in the Western media. This immediately conveys the impression that jihad by definition is war waged for religious reasons, particularly to forcibly replace all other religions with Islam. This understanding is a fundamental distortion of the purposes of the military jihad. A few news outlets and journalists exercise greater responsibility: They take care to translate "jihad" as "struggle" or "effort" and occasionally mention the different ways in which this human struggle is carried out during one's earthly existence.

Specific political and historical circumstances determine what sort of spin the military jihad and its (supposed) practitioners receive in the Western media. Between 1979 and 1989 under a program known as Operation Cyclone, the US government actively supported the group known as the Mujahedeen in Afghanistan who were fighting the Soviet occupation forces there. "Those who carry out jihad" (this is what "Mujahedeen" means in Arabic) were portrayed favorably in the American and European press at that time because they were assumed to be fighting on the right side—that is to say, against the dark forces of communism—and thus serving the interests of Western nations. A James Bond movie titled *The Living Daylights* celebrated the heroic exploits of the Mujahedeen, led by a swashbuckling, Oxford-educated Afghan, who fought shoulder-to-shoulder with British allies against the communist invaders. The Hollywood movie *Rambo III* similarly portrayed the Mujahedeen in a highly favorable light. Jihad carried out at the instigation of Western governments was considered a noble activity. The Western media (and the movie industry) accordingly played along.

Not too long after the Russians were successfully expelled from Afghanistan, some of the Mujahedeen of Afghanistan morphed into the Taliban, the Afghan militia who initiated a reign of austerity, puritanism, and fear in the 1990s. The Taliban promoted the idea of militancy under the rubric of jihad against all those who opposed their brutal policies. "Jihad" now began to be used in the Western media as a reference to the activity of Muslim religious fanatics, opposed to democratic forms of government and intent on destroying Western civilization.

Since the deadly September 11 attacks, the predominant understanding of jihad has become "terrorism" in many quarters in the United States. The word "terrorist" is used almost reflexively in the Western media in connection with acts of violence perpetrated by actors from Muslim backgrounds. In contrast, there is a general reluctance to use the term when the perpetrators are from non-Muslim backgrounds. When the Murrah federal building in Oklahoma City was bombed in 1995, media pundits were quick to say that it had all the hallmarks of "Islamic terrorism" and the ready assumption was that the perpetrators must be "Muslim terrorists." When it was ultimately revealed that the violent act had been carried out by Timothy McVeigh, a homegrown terrorist from a Christian background and a member of the American Patriot

Movement, the public hysteria subsided quite a bit and the word "terrorist" dropped out of media accounts of the event.

This situation bears comparison to the media coverage of the January 6, 2021, mob attack on the US Capitol in Washington, DC, as a response to the 2020 presidential elections that resulted in the victory of Joe Biden. Other than some commentators on liberal outlets like the cable television channel MSNBC, most journalists and "talking heads" covering the insurrection largely refrained from using the term "terrorists," or more specifically "domestic terrorists," to refer to the attackers. In the months following the attack, some Republican members of Congress went so far to paint the mob, whose political allegiances they share, as "peaceful patriots"— these were the exact words of Arizona representative Paul Gozar. Another congressman, Andrew Clyde from Georgia, described the mob attack as a "normal tourist visit!" This was despite that many of these insurrectionists, motivated by their extremist political views, had resorted to unprovoked violence with the express intention of creating an atmosphere of terror for these very same members of Congress. The erection of a gallows on the Capitol grounds, the open calls for the murder of Vice President Mike Pence, and the vicious beating of police officer Michael Fanone left no doubt about their intent to do harm with extreme malice. These acts of militancy and intimidation aimed at a civilian population meet the basic definition of terrorism. The ingrained reluctance on the part of the media and beyond to apply the term "terrorist" to other than militants from a Muslim background points to the ideological motivations behind the selective application of this pejorative term in American public discourses.

Does the American media cover violent acts carried out by Muslims differently than those carried out by non-Muslims?

Academic research has confirmed that the American media spends far more time covering militant acts carried out by perpetrators with Muslim-sounding names than those carried out by non-Muslim perpetrators. This conclusion was reached by researchers at Georgia State University in a study published in 2019 titled "Why Do Some Terrorist Attacks Receive More Media Attention Than Others?" The study provides compelling evidence that terror attacks carried out by Muslims receive more than five times as much media coverage as those carried out by non-Muslims in the United States. Analysis of coverage of all terrorist attacks in the United States between 2011 and 2015 led to the discovery that there was a 449 percent increase in media attention when the attacker was a Muslim. Muslims committed just 12.4 percent of attacks during the period under consideration but received 41.4 percent of the news coverage.

The researchers who conducted the survey studied US newspaper coverage of every terrorist attack on American soil and counted the total number of articles dedicated to each attack. They found that the 2013 Boston Marathon bombing, carried out by Tamerlan and Dzhokhar Tsarnaev, two Chechen Muslim attackers originally from Kyrgyzstan (in Central Asia), and where three people were killed, received almost 20 percent of all coverage related to US terror attacks in the five-year period. In contrast, reporting of a 2012 massacre at a Sikh temple in Wisconsin that left six people dead and was carried out by Wade Michael Page—a Caucasian man from a Christian background—received just 3.8 percent of coverage. Dylann Roof, who is also white and Christian, shot to death nine people at an African American church in Charleston, South Carolina, in 2015 but received only 7.4 percent of media coverage. Similarly, a 2014 attack by Frazier Glenn Miller, a Euro-American, on a Kansas synagogue that left three dead in its wake accounted for just 3.3 percent of reports.

All of these attacks meet widely-used definitions of terrorism, according to these researchers. Such findings clearly suggest that the media helps make people disproportionately fearful of Muslims as terrorists. Overreporting of terrorist attacks carried out by perpetrators from Muslim backgrounds contributes to popular perceptions that Muslims are inherently violent. The frequent framing of such violent acts as religiously motivated further contributes to the perception that Islamic teachings condone arbitrary acts of terror under the cover of jihad.

How does Hollywood portray jihad and Muslims?

An illuminating book by Jack Shaheen, *Reel Bad Arabs: How Hollywood Vilifies a People*, provides plenty of documentation that, wittingly or unwittingly, a considerable number of Hollywood producers continue to perpetuate the stereotype that Muslims, especially men, are violent and pose a danger to American society unless restrained by the non-Muslim Euro-American hero. The Muslim anti-hero is often portrayed as "brandishing an automatic weapon, crazy hate in his eyes, Allah on his lips," as Shaheen remarked.

Shaheen meticulously catalogued and examined several popular Hollywood action films and discovered that most of them conformed to such caricatures of Muslim men. They also tended to dehumanize Muslim women and children. Even a children's film like *Aladdin* portrays the Arab world as "barbaric." (The 2019 remake of this film removed some of the more offensive stereotypes in response to the criticism it received for the earlier version, particularly from Arab-American groups like the American-Arab Anti-Discrimination Committee.) As Shaheen phrased it, "The celluloid Arab is the cultural 'other.'" This was brought home dramatically after the release of the movie *Rules of Engagement* in 2000. Toward the conclusion of the movie, there is a scene in which US Marines in Yemen fire on a group of civilians that include women and children. When this scene played in movie theaters across the United States, audiences are reported to have cheered this senseless massacre. Hollywood had so frequently dehumanized Arabs and Muslims that generations of American moviegoers had learned to view them as enemies who deserve to be indiscriminately mowed down.

For its painstaking documentation and level-headed treatment of a highly sensitive topic, Shaheen's work has become a classic. This particular problem—the stereotypical unflattering, often hostile, depictions of Arabs and Muslims in Hollywood films—has by no means disappeared. Shaheen's work remains invaluable for the light it sheds on how the film industry, both overtly and subliminally, affects how a broad segment of the American population views Muslims and understands jihad.

How does the internet affect public perceptions of jihad in the West?

There are many unreliable websites whose sole function is to spread inaccurate and inflammatory information about Islam in general and jihad in particular. These websites are maintained by groups or individuals who are often described as "Islamophobes"—that is to say, they fear and hate Islam and Muslims. These groups and individuals have a vested interest in portraying Islam and Muslims in the worst possible light. Jihad is depicted by them as an unrelenting violent religious obligation that requires Muslims to militarily wipe out or subjugate non-Muslims. Jihad understood in this way is presented by these Islamophobic groups and individuals as the one activity that characterizes Muslims and renders them incapable of peacefully coexisting with other groups of people. Muslims *as Muslims* are innately dangerous, and some go so far as to say that Muslim populations themselves especially in the West, should be wiped out on account of the threat they are assumed to represent. These Islamophobes are in many ways the mirror image of al-Qaeda and ISIS ideologues, who similarly portray (non-Muslim) Westerners as the unrelenting enemy of Muslims everywhere and thus an inherent threat that needs to be eliminated. These two groups feed off each other's feverish rhetoric and confrontational worldview; each needs the other to justify its existence.

One Islamophobic website explains the reason for its existence in the following manner:

> Why Jihad Watch? Because non-Muslims in the West, as well as in India, China, Russia, and the world over, are facing a concerted effort by Islamic jihadists, the motives and goals of whom are largely ignored by the Western media, to destroy their societies and impose Islamic law upon them—and to commit violence to that end even while their overall goal remains out of reach. That effort goes under the general rubric of jihad.

If one knew nothing else about jihad and/or about Muslims in general, one might find such language convincing and frightening to the core. Flooding the website with such sinister depictions of jihad has become the tool of choice for these purveyors of hate. They thus seek to intimidate and disenfranchise Western Muslim citizens and cast a malignant light over all Muslims everywhere.

Are there Western militants who are influenced by Islamophobic rhetoric on jihad?

There are indeed. One individual who found such rhetoric convincing and chose to act on it was a thirty-two-year-old Norwegian man by the name of Anders Breivik. On July 22, 2011, he planted a bomb in an Oslo government building that caused eight fatalities—apparently inspired by Timothy McVeigh's bombing of the Murrah federal building in Oklahoma City sixteen years earlier. A few hours later, Breivik shot and killed sixty-eight people, mostly teenagers, at a Labor Party youth camp on Utoya Island outside Oslo. As happened with McVeigh's act of terrorism, most mainstream media outlets, including the *New York Times*, the *Washington Post*, and *The Atlantic*, immediately jumped to the conclusion that Muslim "jihadists" were behind the attacks, which supposedly bore the imprint of al-Qaeda operatives. By the next day, however, these media outlets were forced to acknowledge that a Nordic-looking man who identified as a Christian conservative had carried out these terrorist attacks.

At his arraignment a few days later in Oslo, Breivik admitted to his crimes and declared that his violence was motivated by a desire to rid Europe of Muslims and destroy what he claimed was an "ongoing Islamic colonization of Europe." The purpose of the attack was to make the Norwegian Labor Party "pay the price" for apparently facilitating a Muslim takeover of Norway. He said he was influenced by the inflammatory rhetoric of the extremist Dutch politician Geert Wilders, who regularly rails against the Muslim presence in Europe, and by the books of the American journalist Bruce Bawer, who lives in Norway and pens hatemongering tracts against Muslims. One of these tracts by Bawer is titled *While Europe Slept: How Radical Islam Is Destroying the West from Within*. In his 1,500-page manifesto, Breivik also liberally provided citations from the blogs of certain American Islamophobic "stars," which routinely proclaim that Islam is waging violent jihad against the West and that Muslims cannot help but be religious fanatics on account of their dangerous beliefs.

Prominent among the bloggers mentioned by Breivik was Robert Spencer, who runs the website titled Jihad Watch (mentioned earlier). Spencer won the dubious distinction of having been mentioned by Breivik the most—162 times—followed by Spencer's collaborator Pamela Geller, who was mentioned about a dozen times. Together they run an outfit called Stop Islamization of America (also known as the American Freedom Defense Initiative), which circulates baseless conspiracy theories about Western Muslims while claiming to fight radicalism. Breivik's frequent references to these individuals and their toxic prose establishes without doubt that the web of misinformation created by these provocateurs had led him to engage in the senseless murderous attacks on innocent civilians in Oslo. Although their blogs had not explicitly called for violence against Muslims, the American Islamophobes referenced by the Norwegian terrorist had created "the infrastructure from which Breivik emerged," as former CIA officer Marc Sageman phrased it in a *New York Times* article published shortly after the shooting.

Anti-Islamic hatemongering is also the province of certain "think tanks," such as the Center for Security Policy, the Middle East Forum, and the Investigative Project on Terrorism, which were also named by Breivik in his manifesto as sources of inspiration. Typically these organizations traffic in sensationalist rhetoric about Islam and Muslims, attempting to whip up public paranoia about "creeping Sharia" and about an assumed worldwide Muslim conspiracy to take over the West through the instrument of militant jihad. As of the writing of this book, rhetoric of this sort has helped to galvanize nativist and xenophobic political opposition to Western Muslims and brought Islamophobic politicians and political parties to power in a number of Western countries, including the United States.

Such rhetoric is not about to go away—the US organizations mentioned earlier are bankrolled by powerful donors, like the Donors Capital Fund, the Russell Berrie Foundation, Lynde and Harry Bradley Foundation, among others. These foundations contribute millions of dollars to Islamophobic organizations. Thanks to their "largesse," such organizations have mounted a very effective campaign against Muslims, agitating against their presence and relentlessly vilifying their religion as one that promotes endless violence in the name of jihad. Some of their hate-mongering rhetoric has been adopted by right-wing Christian and Jewish groups and infiltrated the media—not just Fox News and the *Washington Times*, as might be expected, but also the editorial pages of the *Wall Street*

Journal, for example. What were once dismissed as fringe, extremist views have seeped into the American mainstream and gained a certain legitimacy, especially after the 2016 presidential elections. Peddling hatred against Muslims has become a powerful and profitable industry in contemporary America and Europe.

Words have consequences. Inflammatory rhetoric circulating on the internet and popular media and increasingly adopted by government officials and members of the US Congress have led to a spike in violence against American Muslims. According to the Southern Poverty Law Center, which tracks extremism in the United States, the number of hate groups active in the United States rose for the second year in a row in 2016, propelled in part by the mainstreaming of far-right rhetoric by the Trump presidency, particularly on topics like immigration and Islam. The number of anti-Muslim groups grew the most, almost tripling to 101 in 2016 from thirty-four in 2015. In its annual report, the center said that there were 917 known hate groups operating in the United States in 2016, an increase from 892 in 2015 and 784 in 2014. In the first ten days after Trump's election, the center documented 867 bias incidents, including more than three hundred that targeted immigrants or Muslims.

Mosques remain a tempting target for hate crimes. A report prepared by the American Civil Liberties Union in May 2020 documented eleven or more attacks on mosques in seven states since 2005. Another fourteen states reported between five and ten attacks; the remaining states witnessed between one and four anti-mosque incidents during this period.

A detailed account of prominent Islamophobes and Islamophobic organizations is provided by the Center for American Progress in their 2011 report *Fear, Inc.: The Roots of the Islamophobic Industry in America*; also available at their website (https://www.americanprogress.org).

*How can one challenge anti-Islamic discourses that distort
the meanings of jihad?*

There are a number of academic units, think tanks, and advocacy groups that are proactively seeking to engage and challenge the growing tide of Islamophobia and its poisonous
consequences. The obvious way to undermine the organized,
well-heeled campaigns of disinformation spearheaded by anti-
Islamic groups in the United States is to provide accurate, well-
researched, and well-documented information in its stead and
make such information as accessible as possible to a wide
audience.

One of the newest and most effective initiatives in this
regard has been launched by the Prince Waleed bin Talal
Center for Muslim-Christian Understanding at Georgetown
University in Washington, DC. Called the Bridge Initiative, its
mission statement reads in part as follows:

> It is our view that in order to safeguard our national se-
> curity and uphold America's core values, we must return
> to a fact-based civil discourse regarding the challenges
> we face as a nation and world. . . . A first step toward
> the goal of honest, civil discourse is to expose—and
> marginalize—the influence of the individuals and groups
> who make up the Islamophobia network in America by
> actively working to divide Americans against one an-
> other through misinformation.

Launched in 2015, this Initiative in its short life span has
attracted the attention of those seeking alternatives to the
usual media outlets for balanced and non-sensational, factual
reporting about Muslims in the United States and elsewhere.
A survey of the Bridge Initiative's website reveals that they
constantly monitor popular media outlets and provide regular updates on Islamophobic incidents globally. As part of
their efforts to counter prevailing stereotypes of Muslims as

intrinsically violent and dangerous, the Initiative has compiled
fact sheets and reports focused on historical and scholarly
understandings of jihad. They have also documented the various ways American Muslims and others are challenging radical understandings of politics and religion that are attributed
to them by anti-Islamic activists.

In the United States, American Muslim civil rights and
advocacy groups are at the forefront of efforts to push back
against Islamophobia and allow Muslims to represent themselves in all their diversity. Among such organizations are the
Council on American-Islamic Relations (CAIR), the Muslim
Public Action Committee (MPAC), the Islamic Society of North
America (ISNA), and the Islamic Council of North America
(ICNA), which regularly hold conferences, workshops, and information sessions to challenge Islamophobia; provide repre-
sentation for Muslim citizens in the political and civil spheres;
and advocate for the civil and human rights of American
Muslims when they are violated. A number of these organizations provide internships for undergraduate and graduate
students so that they may learn critical political and lobbying
skills to make them more effective citizens. They also engage in outreach to other religious communities and participate in interfaith activities to promote religious and political
freedom and combat bigotry. They liaise with members of
churches, synagogues, temples, and other houses of worship
and have established broad coalitions with ethnic and special interest groups representing, for example, Americans of
Japanese, Sikh, and Hindu backgrounds—all of whom have
similarly encountered cultural ostracism, racism, and violence. American Muslim groups also work hand in hand
with secular civil rights and legal advocacy groups, such as
the American Civil Liberties Union (ACLU), the Southern
Poverty Law Center, the American Bar Association, and others
to defend their rights as American citizens. CAIR, in particular, keeps track of incidents of discrimination and violence
directed at American Muslims and provides much-needed

counsel to those seeking legal redress against employers, for example, who discriminate against Muslims. These American Muslim organizations have been attacked and defamed by Islamophobic activists, who regularly misrepresent them as a front for what they describe as "a global Muslim Brotherhood" that is intent on launching militant jihad against the West.

Can educational institutions play a role in providing balanced information about jihad?

They certainly can. As educators, mentors, and advisors, schoolteachers and college and university professors can train and are training the next generation of scholars, policymakers, politicians, journalists, social activists, and responsible citizens to develop good habits of critical reading, listening, and reflection. Such habits will help them navigate the barrage of information that confronts them daily and will help them distinguish facts from manufactured news. Students come into classrooms mostly with open minds and an eagerness to learn through critical inquiry and engagement.

You know you are making headway when students learn to thoughtfully analyze and deconstruct what they hear and read in less respectable media outlets and/or on the internet. Recently, one of my students at Indiana University wrote this in her final essay:

If more people, especially those who don't believe the negative things said but don't know enough to make a difference, made an effort to learn about Islam, then I think things might be different. Maybe the bigoted voices wouldn't sound so loud, and maybe the stereotypes would be referred to less. If people made an effort to understand, rather than just repeat the same negative things that they hear, then maybe the world would be a less hateful place.

Academics can also bring their expertise to bear on hot-button issues in the public sphere—such as jihad—challenging uninformed and reflexive views, and encouraging people to rely on evidence-based, factual information. They can publish accessible books for nonspecialist readers who are sometimes skeptical of what they hear and watch on popular media and are anxious for reliable and credible information about Islam and Muslims without fearmongering. A number of academics write op-ed pieces in newspapers and blogs that can be widely distributed on the internet and through social media. Some of them take the time (and should take the time) to cultivate friendships with journalists who are frequently eager to work with them and help get their viewpoints out to the broader public. Others participate in television and radio talk shows, upload YouTube videos of relevant public lectures, and contribute to public fora of many kinds. Such public activities showcase the issues that are at stake today for Muslims as a global community, the overwhelming majority of whom seek to coexist peacefully with the rest of humanity.

One may consider these attempts as part of a collective, nondenominational struggle—that is to say, jihad—against misinformation and to promote better understanding in its place through responsible, engaged scholarship.

GLOSSARY: IMPORTANT NAMES, PLACES, EVENTS, AND TERMS

Notes: The Arabic definite article al- is not part of the alphabetization of names; names are alphabetized according to the first letter after the definite article.

All dates are Common Era (CE).

Abbasids established a dynasty after they overthrew the Umayyads in 750. The Abbasid dynasty was centered in Baghdad, Iraq; it inaugurated a "golden age" of learning, high culture, and prosperity; ruled until 1258 when the Mongols sacked Baghdad.

Abd al-Razzaq al-Sanani (d. 827) compiler of an early hadith work titled *al-Musannaf.*

Abduh, Muhammad (d. 1905) prominent nineteenth-century Egyptian scholar and reformer; co-author, with his student Rashid Rida (d. 1935), of an influential Quran commentary in a modernist vein.

Abu Hanifa (d. 767) a Successor (second-generation Muslim) from Kufa, Iraq, who became a famous jurist. The Hanafi school of law is named after him.

Ahl al-sunna "people who follow the practices and customs of the Prophet"; Sunnis for short, who constitute about 85 percent of the world's roughly 1.8 billion Muslims.

Aisha bint Abi Bakr (d. 614) youngest wife- of Muhammad and daughter of Abu Bakr, the first caliph; was a prolific transmitter of hadith and revered in general for her piety and learning.

al-Andalus refers to Spain under Muslim rule between 711 and 1492.

al-Awzai, Abd al-Rahman (d. 774) prominent jurist from Syria whose views are frequently reported in later legal works. He was one of the teachers of Abd al-Razzaq al-Sanani, the editor of an early hadith collection.

al-Azhar University established in roughly 975 in Cairo, Egypt, as a mosque-university by the Fatimids, a Shii dynasty. After the Sunni Seljuqs gained control of Egypt in 1171, al-Azhar became the premier institution of Sunni religious education.

Allah Arabic name for the one deity worshipped by Muslims; the name existed in the pre-Islamic period as well. Arabic-speaking Christians and Jews also refer to God as Allah.

al-Banna, Jamal (d. 2013) reformer and prolific author, younger brother of Hasan al-Banna who founded the Muslim Brotherhood. Unlike his brother, Jamal al-Banna was known for his socially liberal views and critique of certain classical legal positions.

Battle of Badr first battle fought by Muslims in 624 against the pagan Meccans who had persecuted and attacked them. Quran 22:39 is understood by exegetes to refer to this incident as a justified act of self-defense against Meccan aggression. The battle of Badr is mentioned by name in Quran 3:123.

Battle of Hunayn took place in 630 after the fall of Mecca against two Bedouin tribes who had gathered troops in order to attack Muslims. The battle took place in the valley of Hunayn between Mecca and the city of Taif where these Bedouin tribes launched a surprise ambush upon the Muslim army sent to intercept them. The tribes were eventually defeated. The battle is mentioned in Quran 9:25.

Battle of Khandaq although referred to as a battle, no fighting took place. The event takes its name from the Persian word for "trench" (*khandaq*) that was dug around the city of Medina to protect it from Meccan attack in 627. The Meccan army vainly tried to cross the trench for two weeks, but finally admitted defeat and retreated to Mecca.

Battle of Khaybar conducted in 628 against the Jewish tribe of Banu Nadir in the oasis of Khaybar in the Arabian Peninsula. The Banu Nadir had allied themselves with the pagan Meccans against the Muslims during the Battle of Khandaq; consequently they were exiled to Khaybar by Muhammad. Eager for revenge, the Banu Nadir continued to foment hostilities against the Prophet and goaded neighboring Arab tribes to rise up against him. Finally, the Muslim army laid siege to their fortresses that led to their eventual surrender, after which the Banu Nadir were allowed to continue to live in Khaybar in return for a tribute.

Battle of Tabuk refers to the military expedition led by Muhammad to the Syrian border in 630 when he heard that the Byzantines had amassed their forces there in preparation for an attack on Muslims. Although referred to as a battle, no fighting occurred since the Byzantine forces failed to materialize.

Battle of Uhud took place in 625 against the pagan Meccans who returned in this year to avenge their defeat at Badr.

Breivik, Anders Norwegian Christian militant who carried out terror attacks in 2011 in Oslo as a response to the increasing Muslim presence in Europe.

al-Bukhari (d. 870) compiler of the most famous hadith collection among Sunnis titled *al-Sahih*.

al-Buti, Ramadan (d. 2013) prominent Syrian scholar and author of *Jihad in Islam*.

Companions close associates of the Prophet Muhammad, male and female; all hadiths have to go back to a Companion to be authoritative.

Constitution of Medina a document drawn up by Muhammad immediately after the Emigration to Medina in 622 that described the Meccan Emigrants, Medinan Helpers, and Jews of Medina as constituting one community (*umma*) with equal rights and obligations.

Dar al-Harb a legal term coined by early jurists that referred to the "House/Abode of War," designating territories under non-Muslim control and regarded as a source of threat to the security of Muslim realms.

Dar al-Islam a legal term referring to the "House/Abode of Islam," designating territories under Muslim rule in which Muslim and non-Muslim residents feel secure.

Dar al-Sulh/Ahd a legal term referring to the "Abode of Reconciliation" or "Abode of Treaty" into which non-Muslim polities entered by signing peace treaties with Muslim authorities. The conception of these abodes do not derive either from the Quran or the hadith.

Emigrants Meccan Muslims who emigrated to Medina, called Muhajirun in Arabic.

Fadail literally "virtues," "excellences." The term refers to a genre of literature that praises people, places, and certain actions or attributes, like patience and valor.

Faraj, Muhammad Abd al-Salam (d. 1982) Egyptian radical who assassinated Egyptian president Anwar Sadat in 1982. Author of a book called *The Neglected Duty* (in English translation) in which he asserted that Muslims should violently overthrow their corrupt rulers in the name of jihad. Numerous refutations were composed by mainstream scholars in response.

Fatimid caliphate refers to the Shii dynasty established in Cairo, Egypt, in 909; fell to the Sunni Seljuks in 1171.

Fi sabil allah meaning "in the way of God," "for the sake of God."

Fiqh Islamic jurisprudence or the study of law, the sources of which are the Quran, sunna, consensus, and analogical reasoning.

al-Ghazali, Abu Hamid (d. 1111) famous scholar and theologian of the eleventh century who embraced the mystical Sufi path to knowledge. Author of the renowned work *Revival of the Religious Sciences.*

al-Ghunaimi, Mohammad Talaat modern Egyptian jurist and author of several works comparing Islamic and Western international law.

Hadith refers to the sayings of Muhammad. It is the second source of law and ethics after the Quran.

Hajj annual pilgrimage to the Kaba during the twelfth month of Dhu al-hijja in the Islamic calendar. The pilgrimage season ends with the Feast of Sacrifice (Id al-Adha) that commemorates Abraham's sacrifice of a ram in lieu of his son Ishmael in Mecca.

Harb usual Arabic word for war; not connected to jihad in the Quran.

Helpers Medinan Muslims, called Ansar in Arabic, who provided financial and other forms of assistance to the Meccan Emigrants.

Hijra the emigration to Medina in 622 that corresponds to the first year of the Islamic calendar.

Hiraba refers to brigandage, highway robbery, piracy, or sedition; often translated today as "terrorism." Those who carry out hiraba are called *muharibun* (in today's parlance, "terrorists").

Ibn Abbas (d. ca. 688) a cousin of the Prophet and a prominent Companion, highly regarded for his deep learning, especially his knowledge of the Quran.

Ibn Abi al-Dunya (d. 894) well-known pious scholar from Baghdad who wrote a popular work on religious piety (*zuhd*) and another on patient forbearance (*sabr*).

Ibn Hajar (d. 1449) well-known scholar of hadith and biographical works from the Mamluk period.

Ibn Hanbal, Ahmad (d. 855) famous hadith scholar and jurist from ninth-century Baghdad, after whom the Hanbali school of law is named.

Ibn Qayyim al-Jawziyya (d. 1350) popular Hanbali jurist from Damascus, Syria, who studied with Ibn Taymiyya (see his entry).

Ibn Qudama (d. 1223) Hanbali jurist from Palestine, whose legal work *Kitab al-Mughni (The Indispensable Book)* is widely consulted.

Ibn Taymiyya (d. 1328) famous and controversial Hanbali scholar from the Mamluk period, author of several legal and theological works, often cited by conservative Muslim groups in the modern period.

Ijma refers to the consensus of the Muslim community on critical issues; in reality refers to the consensus of Muslim jurists. It is one of the sources of law in addition to the Quran, sunna, and analogical reasoning.

Ijtihad independent reasoning of the jurists in matters regarding which there is no revealed text.

Imara, Muhammad contemporary Egyptian jurist who is the author of a detailed refutation of militant positions.

Islam refers to an individual's conscious submission and commitment to God's will. The root consonants—*slm*—of the word Islam also generate meanings of peace, peacemaking, and reconciliation. Islam is, furthermore, the name given in the Quran to the original monotheistic religion practiced by Abraham and his descendants and by all the prophets sent by God to humankind.

Jahiliyya term for the pre-Islamic period. Usually translated as "Age of Ignorance"; also understood to refer to an era characterized by recklessness and lack of self-restraint.

Jihad literally: struggle, effort, striving. The longer Arabic term *al-jihad fi sabil allah* means "striving in the path of God" in different spheres of life to promote what is good and just and prevent what is wrong and oppressive.

Jihad al-nafs spiritual struggle, also called in Arabic *al-Jihad al-akbar* (the greater struggle); name given in later literature to the Quranic concept of *sabr*.

Jihad al-sayf literally "struggle of the sword" or armed combat; also called in Arabic *al-jihad al-asghar* (the lesser struggle); name given in later literature to the Quranic concept of *qital*.

Jizya a kind of poll tax levied on Christian and Jewish men who were able to pay it in lieu of military service. Women, children, and the poor among them did not pay this tax. Men from these communities who served in the military were exempt from paying the jizya. In comparison, both Muslim men and women of means paid the wealth tax (*zakat*) to the state treasury. Zakat and jizya funds were used to financially support the poor from among both Muslims and non-Muslims in the early period.

Juma, Ali former chief mufti (jurisconsult) of Egypt; author of *Jihad in Islam*.

Kaba the cube-shaped shrine in Mecca to which adult Muslims, if they are financially and physically capable, should undertake a pilgrimage at least once in their lives. According to Islamic tradition, the Kaba was established by Abraham and his son Ishmael and dedicated to the worship of the one God.

Khan, Wahiduddin (d. 2021) prominent contemporary Indian Muslim peace activist and prolific author.

Kharijites an extremist violent faction that emerged in the late seventh century during the time of the fourth caliph Ali ibn Abi Talib, who was assassinated by one of them in 661. The Kharijites accused other Muslims, who did not subscribe to their extremist views, of having lapsed from Islam. In their view, such "lapsed" Muslims could be fought and killed. Today's Islamist militant groups are frequently compared to the Kharijites.

Kufr refers to the ingratitude of those who deny the bounties of God and deny his existence. Such an ungrateful person is a *kafir* (pl. *kuffar*) and, therefore, an unbeliever.

Malik ibn Anas jurist and author of *al-Muwatta* (*The Well-Trodden Path*), an important early collection of legal hadith; the Maliki school of law is named after him.

Mamluk dynasty established by Turkic slave-warriors in 1250, with their center in Cairo, Egypt; lasted until the rise of the Ottomans in 1517.

al-Mawardi, Abu al-Hasan (d. 1058) prominent Shafii jurist from Baghdad, known for his close ties to the Abbasid rulers. Author of a well-known treatise on governance and statecraft.

Mecca city in present-day Saudi Arabia in which Muhammad was born and where he preached for roughly twelve years.

Meccan period 610–622; refers to the period when the Prophet began receiving revelations in Mecca until his emigration to Medina.

Medina city in present-day Saudi Arabia to which Muhammad emigrated from Mecca to escape the persecution of the pagan Arabs there. Called Yathrib before the emigration to Medina.

Medinan period 622–632; period from after the *hijra* till the death of the Prophet.

Muhammad ibn Abd Allah prophet of Islam, referred to as the Messenger of God (*Rasul Allah* in Arabic). Born in Mecca circa 570, he died in Medina in 632 when he was about sixty-three years old.

Musannaf a hadith collection in which its content is arranged according to subject matter.

Muslim one who knowingly and sincerely submits to the one God. The Quran uses this term to refer to specifically the followers of the Prophet Muhammad, as well as all monotheistic worshippers through time.

Muslim ibn Hajjaj (d. 875) commonly referred to in short as Muslim; compiler of "sound" or reliable hadiths in a collection known as *al-Sahih*; ranked second to al-Bukhari's work with the same title.

Naskh controversial concept of "abrogation," according to which certain early verses in the Quran are considered by some scholars to be cancelled or superseded by later verses.

Peace Verse a name given in this volume to Quran 8:61 that exhorts Muslims to make peace with an adversary that seeks peace. This commandment is understood to be valid and binding for Muslims for all time and places by major scholars; a few, however, considered it to be abrogated by Quran 9:5.

People of the Book used in the Quran to refer to Jews, Christians, and Sabians (an early monotheistic group) who enjoy protection of life, property, and religion in Islamic realms, usually upon payment of the jizya.

Protected People the Arabic term is *ahl al-dhimma*; singular *dhimmi*. This designation overlaps to some degree with the concept of the People of the Book. In addition to Jews, Christians, and Zoroastrians, this protected status was later extended to Hindus, Buddhists, and others as well.

Qital fighting, armed combat, a conditional aspect of jihad; called the "lesser jihad" or "struggle by the sword" in extra-Quranic literature.

Quran the central scripture of Islam; according to Islamic doctrine, it is a faithful transcript of God's revelations in Arabic to the Prophet Muhammad in the seventh century.

Quran commentators (select famous ones mentioned in this work) Mujahid ibn Jabr (d. 722); Muqatil ibn Sulayman (d. 767); al-Tabari (d. 923); al-Zamakhshari (d. 1144); Fakhr al-Din al-Razi (d. 1210); al-Qurtubi (d. 1273); Ibn Kathir (d. 1373).

Quraysh prominent Meccan tribe into which Muhammad was born, many of whose powerful members opposed and fought the Muslims until Mecca surrendered peacefully in 630.

Qutb, Sayyid (d. 1966) modern Egyptian revolutionary thinker executed by Egyptian president Gamal Abd al-Nasser. His works are still consulted by contemporary militant groups.

Rightly Guided Caliphs refers to the first four leaders of the Muslim community: Abu Bakr (d. 634); Umar (d. 644); Uthman (d. 656); and Ali (d. 661). Called Rightly Guided because they governed according to Islamic ideals, particularly in having practiced *shura* or consultation with the people they ruled over.

Sabr can be translated as patient forbearance, fortitude, endurance, perseverance. It is the constant feature of jihad; later called the greater jihad or "spiritual struggle" in extra-Quranic literature.

Sahih refers to a hadith considered "sound"—that is, free of defects in primarily the chain of transmission that contains the names of the transmitters. It is also the title of the famous hadith collections of al-Bukhari and Muslim.

Said, Jawdat prominent contemporary Syrian peace activist and prolific author.

al-Sarakhsi, Muhammad ibn Ahmad (d. ca. 1090) major Hanafi jurist from Transoxiana (Central Asia), author of the well-known Hanafi legal manual titled *Kitab al-Mabsut* (*The Comprehensive Book*).

Schools of law (Sunni) Hanafi, Maliki, Shafii, Hanbali.

al-Shafii, Muhammad ibn Idris (d. 820) influential jurist from Baghdad who later moved to Cairo; the Shafii school of law is named after him.

Shaheen, Jack (d. 2017) author of the acclaimed book *Reel Bad Arabs*, which details violent and demeaning stereotypes of Arabs and Muslims prevalent in the American film industry.

Shahid an eye or legal witness in the Quran; in later non-Quranic usage, a martyr in the nonmilitary and military sense.

Sharia literally meaning "the path to a watering-hole"; refers to revealed ethical, moral, and legal principles known from the Quran and sunna of the Prophet. Human interpretations of the Sharia generate legal rulings that are part of *fiqh* (Islamic jurisprudence), although Sharia itself is often translated into English as "Islamic Law."

al-Shaybani, Muhammad (d. 805) early influential Hanafi jurist from Iraq who studied with Abu Hanifa. He is considered the founder of Islamic international law in the eighth century.

Shia short for Shiat Ali, the supporters of Ali who constitute about 10– 15 percent of the world's approximately 1.8 billion Muslims today.

Shirk refers to polytheism or the worship of many deities. One who is a polytheist is a *mushrik*. The pre-Islamic Arabs are described in the Quran as polytheists who worshipped multiple idols.

Siyar refers to Islamic law of nations or Islamic international law, which regulates relations between Muslim and non-Muslim polities.

Sunna refers to the reported practices, customs, and sayings of Muhammad.

Successors refers to the second generation of Muslims, many of whom transmitted hadiths from the Companions.

Sword Verse a name given in the later period to Quran 9:5 that commanded Muslims in the seventh century to fight and kill the hostile pagan Meccans who had attacked and persecuted them. Some scholars hold the highly controversial position that this verse had abrogated the numerous peaceful verses in the Quran, a position vigorously contested by others.

Tafsir refers to Quran commentary or exegesis, a very rich genre of Islamic literature.

Tawhid refers to belief in one God; monotheism.

Treaty of al-Hudaybiyya signed in 628 between Muhammad and his Meccan adversaries which established a truce for ten years; two years later (630), the Meccans violated the terms of the treaty.

Twelver Shia the largest Shii group who follow twelve religious leaders (Imams) after the Prophet; known in Arabic as the Ithna Ashariyya or Imamiyya.

Umayyads established the first dynasty in Islam after the end of the Rightly Guided caliphate, with their capital in Damascus, Syria; ruled between 661 and 750; widely regarded as illegitimate for instituting dynastic rule.

Umm Salama (d. ca. 680) wife of Muhammad, known for her piety and charity; transmitted many hadiths.

Umm Umara (death date unknown) also known as Nusayba bint Kab. She was one of the earliest converts to Islam in Mecca; became famous for her uncommon valor on the battlefield, particularly during the battle of Uhud in 625. She transmitted hadiths from Muhammad.

Umra a shortened form of the annual pilgrimage (hajj) that can be performed at any time of the year.

al-Zuhayli, Wahba (d. 2015) well-known Syrian jurist who wrote influential works on Islamic international law.

BIBLIOGRAPHY

(only English language sources have been included)

Abdel Haleem, M. A. S. "The *Jjzya* Verse (Q. 9:29): Tax Enforcement on
Non-Muslims in the First Muslim State." *Journal of Qur'anic Studies*
14, no. 2 (2012): 72–89.

Abou El-Fadl, Khaled. *Rebellion and Violence in Islamic Law.*
Cambridge: Cambridge University Press, 2001.

Abou El-Fadl, Khaled. "The Rules of Killing at War." *The Muslim World*
89, no. 2 (April 1999): 144–157.

Afsaruddin, Asma. "The Concept of Peace in Islam." In *The Concept of
Peace in Judaism, Christianity, and Islam*, edited by Georges Tamer,
99–157. Berlin: De Gruyter, 2020.

Afsaruddin, Asma. *The First Muslims: History and Memory.*
Oxford: Oneworld, 2008.

Afsaruddin, Asma. "The Hermeneutics of Inter-Faith
Relations: Retrieving Moderation and Pluralism as Universal
Principles in Qur'anic Exegeses." *Journal of Religious Ethics* 37
(2009): 331–354.

Afsaruddin, Asma. "Jihad, Gender, and Religious Minorities in the *Siyar*
Literature: The Diachronic View." *Studia Islamica* 114 (2019): 1–26.

Afsaruddin, Asma. "Jihad in the Qur'an." In *The Oxford Handbook on
Qur'anic Studies*, edited by Mohammad Abdel Haleem and Mustafa
Shah, 512–526. Oxford: Oxford University Press, 2020.

Afsaruddin, Asma. "Martyrdom in Islam: A Historical Survey."
In *Terrorism, Martyrdom, and Religion: European Perspectives in
Global Context*, edited by Dominic Janes and Alex Houen, 40–58.
Oxford: Oxford University Press, 2014.

Afsaruddin, Asma. "The *Siyar* Laws of Aggression: Juridical Re-
interpretations of Qur'anic *Jihad* and Their Contemporary
Implications for International Law." In *Islam and International
Law: Engaging Self-Centrism from a Plurality of Perspectives*, edited
by Marie-Luisa Frick and Andreas Th. Müller, 45–63. Leiden: Brill/
Martinus Nijhoff, 2013.

Afsaruddin, Asma. *Striving in the Path of God: Jihad and Martyrdom in
Islamic Thought.* Oxford: Oxford University Press, 2013.

Afsaruddin, Asma. "The 'Upright Community': Interpreting
the Righteousness and Salvation of the People of the Book
in the Qur'ān." In *Jewish-Muslim Relations in Past and
Present: A Kaleidoscopic View*, edited by Josef Meri, 48–69. Leiden: E.
J. Brill, 2017.

Ayoub, Mahmoud. *Redemptive Suffering in Islam.* The
Hague: Mouton, 1978.

Bail, Christopher. *Terrified: How Anti-Muslim Fringe Organizations Became
Mainstream.* Princeton: Princeton University Press, 2016.

Blankinship, Khalid Yahya. *The End of the Jihad State: The Reign of Hisham
ibn Abd al-Malik and the Collapse of the Umayyads.* Albany: State
University of New York Press, 1994.

Broisard, Marcel. "On the Probable Influence of Islam on Western
Public and International Law." *International Journal of Middle East
Studies* 11 (1980): 429–450.

Brown, Jonathan. *Hadith: Muhammad's Legacy in the Medieval and Modern
World.* Oxford: Oneworld, 2009.

Choueiri, Youssef. *Islamic Fundamentalism.* London: Pinter, 1990.

Cole, Juan. *Muhammad: Prophet of Peace Amid the Clash of Empires.*
New York: Nation Books, 2018.

Al-Dawoody, Ahmed. *The Islamic Law of War: Justifications and
Regulations.* New York: Palgrave Macmillan, 2011.

De la Rasilla del Moral, Ignacio. "In Search of the Lost
Influence: Islamic Thinkers and the Spanish Origins of International
Law." In *International Law and Islam*, edited by Ignacio de la Rasilla
del Moral and Ayesha Shahid, 146–164. Leiden: Brill/Nijhoff, 2018.

Easwaran, Eknath. *Nonviolent Soldier of Islam, Badshah Khan: A Man to
Match His Mountains.* 2nd ed. Tomales, CA: Nilgiri Press, 1999.

Esposito, John L. *Unholy War: Terror in the Name of Islam.* Oxford: Oxford
University Press, 2002.

Fadel, Mohammad. "International Law, Regional
Developments: Islam." In *Max Planck Encyclopedia of Public*

International Law. Heidelberg: Max Planck Institute for Comparative
Public Law and International Law, 2010. Available at https://
opil.ouplaw.com/view/10.1093/law:epil/9780199231690/
law-9780199231690-e711?rskey=ixD4Fb&result=2&prd=OPIL.

Al-Ghazali, Abu Hamid. *Ihya Ulu m al-Din (The Revival of the Religious
Sciences)*. Translated into English by Mohammad Mahdi al-Sharif.
Beirut: Dar al-kutub al-ilmiyya, 2008.

Al-Ghunaimi, Mohammad Talaat. *The Muslim Conception of International
Law and the Western Approach*. The Hague: Martin Nijhoff, 1968.

Green, Todd. *The Fear of Islam: An Introduction to Islamophobia in the West*.
Minneapolis: Fortress Press, 2015.

Hartigan, Richard Shelly. "Noncombatant Immunity: Reflections on Its
Origins and Present Status." *The Review of Politics* 29 (1967): 204–220.

Hashmi, Sohail, ed. *Jihad, Just Wars and Holy Wars: Christian, Jewish,
and Muslim Encounters and Exchanges*. Oxford: Oxford University
Press, 2012.

Hashmi, Sohail. "Saving and Taking Life in War: Three Modern Muslim
Views." In *The Islamic Ethics of Life: Abortion, War, and Euthanasia*,
edited by Jonathan Brockopp, 129–154. Columbia: University of
South Carolina Press, 2003.

Hillenbrand, Carole. *The Crusades: Islamic Perspectives*.
Edinburgh: Edinburgh University Press, 1999.

Huda, Qamar-ul. *Crescent and Dove: Peace and Conflict Resolution in Islam*.
Washington, DC: United States Institute of Peace Press, 2010.

Jackson, Sherman. "Domestic Terrorism in the Islamic Legal Tradition."
Muslim World 91 (2001): 293–310.

Jackson, Sherman. "Jihad and the Modern World." *Islamic Law and
Culture* 1 (2002): 1–26.

Jansen, Johannes J. G. *The Neglected Duty: The Creed of Sadat's
Assassins and Islamic Resurgence in the Middle East*.
New York: Macmillan, 1986.

Johansen, Robert. "Radical Islam and Nonviolence: A Case Study of
Religious Empowerment and Constraint among Pashtuns." *Journal
of Peace Research* 34 (1997): 53–71.

Kearns, Erin M., Allison E. Betus, and Anthony F. Lemieux. "Why
Do Some Terrorist Attacks Receive More Media Attention Than
Others?" *Justice Quarterly* 36 (2019): 985–1022.

Kelsay, John, and James Turner Johnson, eds. *Just War and
Jihad: Historical and Theoretical Perspectives on War and Peace in
Western and Islamic Traditions*. Greenwood Press: New York 1991.

Khadduri, Majid. *The Islamic Law of Nations: Shaybani's* Siyar.
Baltimore: Johns Hopkins University Press, 1966.

Khalil, Mohammad Hassan. *Jihad, Radicalism, and the New Atheism.*
Cambridge: Cambridge University Press, 2018.

Khan, Wahiduddin. *The True Jihad: The Concept of Peace, Tolerance and
Non-Violence.* New Delhi: Goodword Books, 2002.

Peters, Rudolph. *Jihad in Classical and Modern Islam: A Reader.*
Princeton: Markus Weiner, 1996.

Pape, Robert A. *Dying to Win: The Strategic Logic of Suicide Terrorism.*
New York: Random House, 2005.

Qadi, Wadad. "Non-Muslims in the Muslim Conquest Army in Early
Islam." In *Christians and Others in the Umayyad State,* edited by Antoine
Borrut and Fred M. Donner, 83–128. Chicago: Oriental Institute, 2016.

Qutb, Sayyid. *Milestones.* New Delhi: Islamic Book Service, 2006.

Renard, John. "*Al-Jihad al-Akbar*: Notes on a Theme in Islamic
Spirituality." *The Muslim World* 78 (1988): 225–42.

Roy, Olivier. *Jihad and Death: The Global Appeal of Islamic State.* Translated
by Cynthia Schoch. New York: Oxford University Press, 2017.

Said, Edward. *Covering Islam: How the Media and the Experts Determine
How We See the Rest of the World.* New York: Vintage Books, 1997.

Said, Edward. *Orientalism.* New York: Vintage, 1979.

Said, Jawdat. *Non-Violence: The Basis of Settling Disputes in Islam.*
Translated by Munzer A. Absi, H. Hilwani, and Anas Rifa'i.
Damascus: Dar al-Fikr, 2002.

Salaymeh, Lena. *The Beginnings of Islamic Law: Late Antique Islamicate
Legal Traditions.* Cambridge: Cambridge University Press, 2016.

Satha-Anand, C., G. Paige, and S. Gilliat, eds. *Islam and Non-Violence.*
Honolulu: University of Hawaii Press, 1993.

Shaheen, Jack. *Reel Bad Arabs: How Hollywood Vilifies a People.*
Northampton, MA: Olive Branch Press, 2009.

Shane, Scott. "Killings in Norway Spotlight Anti-Muslim Thought in
US." *New York Times,* July 24, 2011, https://www.nytimes.com/
2011/07/25/us/25debate.html?_r=1.

Siddiqui, Sohaira. "Beyond Authenticity: ISIS and the Islamic
Legal Tradition." *Jadaliyya,* February 24, 2015, https://
www.jadaliyya.com/Details/31825.

Sonn, Tamara. *Is Islam an Enemy of the West?* Malden, MA: Polity
Press, 2016.

Tahir-ul-Qadri, Muhammad. *Fatwa on Suicide Bombings & Terrorism,*
2010, https://www.minhajbooks.com/english/book/376/Fatwa-
on-Terrorism-and-Suicide-Bombings/.

INDEX

For the benefit of digital users, indexed terms that span two pages (e.g., 52–53) may, on occasion, appear on only one of those pages.

Frequently-occurring words and terms like Islam, Muslim(s), Quran (except for specific verses) and hadith are not listed in the index. Names and words beginning with the Arabic definite article *al-* should be looked up under the first consonant after al-.

Abadi, Houda, 152
Abbasid
   caliphate, 90
   elite, 82–83
   period, 83–84, 88, 169
Abd Allah al-Najdi,
   113–14
Abd al-Razzaq al-Sanani, 11–12,
   61–62, 63
Abduh, Muhammad, 32, 36–37,
   91, 134–35, 140, 168
Abode of Islam, 88, 89–90, 139–40,
   169, See also *Dar al-Islam*
Abode of War, 88, 90, 169, See also
   Dar al-Harb
Abode/House of Islam, 5, See
   also Dar al-Islam
Abode/House of War, 5. *See also*
   Dar al-Harb
Abode of Reconciliation, 88, 90,
   See also *Dar al-Sulh*

Abode of Treaty, 88, 89–90, See
   also *Dar al-Ahd*
Abraham, 19–20
abrogation, 3–4, 82, 83–84, 133–34,
   140, See also *naskh*
Abu Bakr, 29–30, 71–72
Abu Bakr al-Baghdadi, 82, 93
Abu Bakr al-Naji, 71–72, 129–30
Abu Basir al-Tartusi, 127
Abu Daud, 60–61
Abu Hanifa, 77, 78–79, 88
Abu Muhammad al-Adnani, 130
Abu Salama ibn Abd al-Rahman, 13
Abu Yusuf, 77
Abul Kalam Azad, Maulana, 152
Abu-Nimer, Muhammad, 152
Abyssinia, 15, 99
Adam, 157–58
Afghanistan, 125, 170–71
Aisha, 85–86, 156
Aladdin, 174–75

Al-Albani, Muhammad, 143
Ali ibn Abi Talib, 29–30, 64–65,
    103–4, 115
alladhina qutilu fi sabil allah, 41–42
American Bar Association, 181–82
American Civil Liberties Union,
    179, 181–82
American Freedom Defense
    Initiative. *See* Stop
    Islamization of America
American Patriot
    Movement, 171–72
American University, 152
Amr ibn al-As, 40
Anas ibn Malik, 43
al-Andalus, 39
Aquinas, Thomas, 164
Arab-Israeli wars, 112
The Atlantic, 176–77
Augustine, bishop of Hippo, 164
Averroes. *See* Ibn Rushd
awliya, 33–34, 85–86, 168–69
al-Awzai, 86
ayat al-sayf, 28. *See also* sword verse
al-Azhar University, 91, 125, 138,
    141, 156–57
Azzam, Abdullah, 125

Badshah Khan. *See* Khan, Syed
    Abd al-Ghaffar
Baghdad, 26, 103, 105, 120–21
al-Baladhuri, 40
al-Banna, Hasan, 115–16, 168–69
al-Banna, Jamal, 168–69
battle of Badr, 17–18
battle of Khandaq. *See* Battle of
    the Trench
battle of Khaybar, 86
battle of the Trench, 155
battle of Uhud, 85–86
Bawer, Bruce, 177
bellum justum, 164. *See also*
    just war
Biden, Joe, 172

Bin Laden, Usama, 124–26, 141
Boko Haram, 93
Boston Marathon, 173
Breivik, Anders, 176–78
Bridge Initiative, 180
Buddhists, 29–30
bughat, 92–93, 115
al-Bukhari, Muhammad, 49–50,
    52, 53–54, 55–56, 58–59, 61,
    62, 63, 64, 65, 66–67, 74, 75,
    76, 101, 149, 156
al-Buti, Muhammad Said
    Ramadan, 138–41
Byzantine Christians, 30–31
Byzantines, 30, 79, 87–88, 90

Cain and Abel, 157
Cairo, 90, 91, 115–16, 125,
    141, 156–57
Carrel, Alexis, 118–19
Center for Security Policy, 178
Charlemagne, 90
Charleston, South Carolina, 173
Chicago, 163
China, 176
Christian gospels, 107
Christian liberation theologies, 117
Cicero, 164
Clyde, Andrew, 172
Companion(s), 36, 37–38, 39,
    43, 47, 51, 52, 54–55, 60–61,
    65–66, 67–68, 75, 85–86, 87,
    114–15, 151, 158
Congress (US), 172, 179
Constantine V, 79
Constitution of Medina, 139–41
Cordoba, Spain, 90
Council on American-Islamic
    Relations (CAIR), 163, 181–82
crusade, 130, 163–64
    Fourth, 38–39
    Third, 38–39
Crusader
    armies, 28, 82–83

attacks, 39
onslaughts, 28–29
Crusaders, 28–29, 87–88
Crusades, 39, 135

Dabiq, 130
Daesh, 129–30
Al-Dahhak, 27
Damascus University, 138
Dar al-Ahd, 88. See also Abode
    of Treaty
Dar al-Islam, 5, 88. See also
    Abode/House of Islam
Dar al-Harb, 5, 88, 168–69. See also
    Abode/House of War
Dar al-salam, 149
Dar al-Sulh, 88. See also Abode of
    Reconciliation
al-Darimi, 67
Dariyya, 114
Day of Judgment, 53, 54–55
Day of Resurrection, 120
De Jure Belli ac Pacis, 164
De Las Casas, Bartolome, 165
De Vitoria, Francisco, 165
Donors Capital Fund, 178–79

Egypt, 111–12, 113–14, 115–16
Egyptian Ministry of
    Education, 115–16
emigration, 9, 15, 17–18, 35, 42–43,
    54, 73, 99, 100, 138–40, 155,
    See also hijra
Emigrant(s), 42–43, 99, 139–40.
    See also Meccan Emigrants;
    Muhajirun
Ethiopia, 15, 99
Ethiopians, 82

Fadail, 49, 60–61, 94, 103
Fahmideh, Mohammed
    Hossein, 126
Faraj, Muhammad Abd al-Salam,
    119–22, 136–38, 168–69

Al-Farida al-ghaiba, 119
fasad, 45
Fatimid caliphate, 90
al-Fazari, Ibrahim, 75
Fear, Inc.: The Roots of the
    Islamophobic Industry in
    America, 179
Federal Bureau of Investigation
    (FBI), 92
fi sabil allah, 5, 11, 41–42, 51
fiqh, 88–89
fitna, 34–36
Fox News, 178–79
Francis I of France, 90
futuh, 40

Gandhi, Mahatma, 154
Geller, Pamela, 177–78
Geneva Conventions, 167
    Additional Protocols, 167
Georgetown University, 180
Georgia, 172
Georgia State University, 172–73
Germanikeia, 79
al-Ghazali, Abu Hamid
    Muhammad, 105–7, 109
ghazawat, 13–14
al-Ghunaimi, Muhammad Talaat,
    32, 169
ghuraf, 54
Golan Heights, 156–57
Gozar, Paul, 172
Greeley, Colorado, 115–16
Grotius, Hugo, 164–65, 166
guardian jurist, 122–23
Gulen, Fethullah, 151–52
Gulf wars, 112–13

hadith
    daif, 49
    gharib, 55–56
    hasan, 48
    sahih, 48
    seventy-two virgins, 61–62

hajj, 19–20, 50
Hamas, 126
Hanafi school of law, 88, 89–90
Hapsburgs, 90
harb, 11
Harun al-Rashid, 90
Harvard, 162
Harvard Crimson, 162
al-Hasan al-Basri, 35–37, 77, 78–
    79, 95–96, 104
head tax, 29–30
hijra, 9, 35, 54, 138–39
Hindu(s), 153–54, 181–82
hiraba, 92–93
holy war, 7, 23, 25–26, 113, 130,
    163–64, 170
  cosmic, 6, 25–26, 130
Huda, Qamarul, 152

Ibn Abbas, 20, 67–68
Ibn Abd al-Barr, 67–68, 92–93
Ibn Abd al-Wahhab,
    Muhammad, 113–15
Ibn Abi al-Dunya, 103, 104, 105
Ibn Abi Rabah, Ata, 37–39, 41, 78–
    79, 80, 81–82
Ibn Atiyya, 14
Ibn Hajar, 55–56, 66, 76
Ibn Hanbal, Ahmad, 55–56, 66–67,
    77, 80, 121, 156
Ibn Hazm, 68–69
Ibn Jurayj, 37–38
Ibn Kathir, 27, 28–29, 39
Ibn Maja al-Qazwini, 55
Ibn al-Mubarak, 14–15
Ibn Naqib al-Misri, Ahmad, 82–83
Ibn Qayyim al-Jawziyya, 108–
    10, 122
Ibn Qudama, 78, 82
Ibn Rushd, 82
Ibn Saud, Muhammad, 113–14
Ibn Taymiyya, 66, 108, 120–21
Ibn Umar, Abd Allah, 37–38, 41
ijtihad, 88–89

Imam, 123, 124
Imamiyya, 64–65
Imara, Muhammad, 136–38, 140
India, 151, 154–55, 176
Indiana University, 182
international law, 7–8, 32, 75,
    84–85, 88–89, 94, 108, 164–65,
    167, 169–70
Investigative Project on
    Terrorism, 178
Iran, 64–65, 105, 113–14, 122–24, 126
Iran-Iraq war, 126
Iranian Revolution, 64–65
Iraq, 64–65, 93, 113–14, 122–23,
    126, 129–30
Ishmael, 19–20
ISIS, 93, 129–30, 146
Islamic Centre in New
    Delhi, 154–55
Islamic Council of North America
    (ICNA), 181–82
Islamic law of nations, 7–8, 85,
    88–89, 165–66
Islamic Society of North America
    (ISNA), 181–82
Islamic State of Iraq and Syria,
    93, 129–30
Islamophobes, 26, 175–76, 177–
    78, 179
Islamophobic
    organizations, 178–79
    website(s), 3, 176
Ismail ibn Ayyash, 62
Israel, 106, 112, 119, 126, 129
Ithna Ashariyya, 64–65

Jahanbegloo, Ramin, 152
Jahiliyya, 118–19
Jamaat-i Islami, 154–55
James Bond movie, 170–71
Jerusalem, 28–29
Jesus, the son of Mary, 107
(al-)Jihad
    al-akbar, 100, 102, 123–24

al-asghar, 100
combative, 1–2, 109, 113, 117,
   120, 121–22, 138–39, 142–
   43, 160–61
external/physical, 65–66
fi sabil allah, 5, 11
greater and lesser, 65–66, 102
greater, spiritual, 100
ideology, 113–14
internal, 4, 122
kabir, 14, 102, 139
lesser, physical, 102
military, 1–2, 3, 5, 7–8, 19–20,
   22–23, 25–26, 28–29, 35–36,
   37–38, 39, 40–41, 49, 50, 51–
   53, 54–55, 58, 60–61, 64–65,
   70–71, 73, 80–83, 84–86, 87,
   91–92, 95, 98, 109, 114–15,
   116–17, 119–20, 121, 123, 129–
   30, 133–34, 139, 142–43, 146–
   47, 153, 158, 164, 170–71
al-nafs, 6, 100, 123–24
noncombative, 12–13, 49, 100,
   101, 102, 139
of the tongue, 102
al-sayf, 100
spiritual, 4, 12–13, 100–1, 102–3,
   109, 122
jihad al-nafs/al-jihad al-
   akbar, 123–24
al-jihad fi al-islam, 138
Jihad in Islam, 138, 141
Jihad Watch, 176, 177–78
jihadi/jihadist, 93, 176–77
jizya, 29–31, 71, 78, 83–84
Juma, Ali, 141–43
jus in bello, 164–65, 166
just conduct, 164. *See also* jus
   in bello
just peace, 140–41
just war, 164

Kaba, 19–20, 36–37
Kadayifci-Orellana, Ayse, 152

Kahramanmarash, 79
Khadduri, Majid, 84–85
Khalid ibn al-Walid, 40
Khan, Syed Abd al-Ghaffar, 151–
   52, 153–55
Khan, Wahiduddin, 151–52, 154–
   55, 156, 160–61
Kharijites, 115, 137–38
Khomein, 122–23
Khomeini, Ayatollah Ruhollah,
   122–24, 126
Khudai Khidmatgars, 151, 153–54
King Abdulaziz University, 125
Kitab al-jihad wa al-siyar, 84–85
Kyrgyzstan, 173

The Lapsed Duty, 119, 136, 168–69
Latin America, 117
Law of War and Peace, 164
Lebanon, 140–41
Leninism, 118
Letter to al-Baghdadi, 146
The Living Daylights, 170–71
Lynde and Harry Bradley
   Foundation, 178–79

Malik ibn Anas, 57, 58, 73, 77
Mamluk period, 19, 28, 39, 87–88
man qutila fi sabil allah, 41–42
The Management of
   Savagery, 129–30
Marash, 79
martyr
   combative, 1–2
   military, 41–42, 44, 57, 58–59,
      60–62, 67, 76–77, 98–99,
      104, 105
martyrdom, 41–42, 44, 57, 58, 59–
   61, 63, 64–65, 68
   military, 42, 44, 58–59, 60–
      61, 64–65
   noncombative, 12–13, 58
   operations, 126, 127–29
Marxist/socialist theories, 117

al-Mawardi, 81–83, 86, 89, 91–92
al-Mawdudi, Abu al-Ala, 115–16,
    123–24, 154–55
McVeigh, Timothy, 171–72, 176–77
Mecca, 9, 18–20, 27, 35, 36–37, 40,
    54, 56, 62, 139–40, 155
Meccan Emigrants, 43, 139. *See
    also* Emigrants; Muhajirun
media, 173
    American, 174
    Western, 171–172
Medina, 9, 15, 17–18, 29–30, 35,
    39–40, 54, 62, 73, 99, 100, 113–
    14, 138–40, 155
Medinan Helpers, 139–40
Middle East Forum, 178
migration, 9
Miller, Frazier Glenn, 173
Mongol
    armies, 82–83
    invasions, 39
Mongols, 88, 120–21
Moses, 159–60
MSNBC, 172
Muhajirun, 42–43. *See
    also* Emigrants;
    Meccan Emigrants
Muhammad, Prophet, 47–48, 50–
    51, 52, 53–54, 55, 56, 57, 58,
    59–62, 65–66, 68–69, 70–75,
    79, 85–88, 91, 99, 101, 102,
    103–4, 121, 133, 139–42, 149,
    155, 156, 158
Muheideen, Qader. *See* Satha-
    Anand, Chaiwat
Mujahedeen, 170–71
mujahid, 66–67, 156
Mujahid ibn Jabr, 20, 21, 30–31, 80
mujahidin, 17
Muqatil ibn Sulayman, 14–15, 18–
    19, 21, 80
murabata, 110. See also *ribat*
Murrah (federal) building, 171–
    72, 176–77

musabara, 95–96, 97
al-Musannaf, 11–12, 61–62, 63
Muslim Brotherhood, 111–12, 115–
    16, 181–82
Muslim (ibn Hajjaj), 53–55, 59,
    66–67, 101
Muslim Public Action Committee
    (MPAC), 181–82
Muslim Spain, 39. *See also*
    al-Andalus
al-Muwatta, 57, 58
MyJihad, 163
mysticism, 103. *See also* Sufism

Najaf, 122–23
al-Nasai, 54
naskh, 3–4, 133–34. *See also*
    abrogation
Nasser, Gamal Abdel, 115–16, 119
Negus, 99
New Delhi, 154–55
New York Times, 176–78
nonviolence, 134, 142–43, 149–50,
    151, 152, 155, 156–57, 160–61
*Non-Violence: The Basis of Settling
    Disputes in Islam*, 157–58
Northwest Frontier Province,
    151, 153
Norwegian Labor Party, 176–77
Nuremberg Charter of 1945, 167

Oklahoma City, 171–72, 176–77
Operation Cyclone, 170–71
Organization of Islamic
    Cooperation (OIC), 169–70
    Charter, 169–70
Orientalists, 26, 100–1
Oslo, 176–78
Ottoman rulers, 90

pacifism, 149–50
    conditional, 150
pacificism, 150
Page, Michael Wade, 173

Pakistan, 151, 153, 154
Palestine, 126
Pashtun(s), 151, 153–54
patient forbearance, 5, 7, 12–13,
    15, 17, 66, 94–99, 100, 103,
    104, 105, 106–7, 108–9, 151
*Patient Forbearance and the Rewards
    For It*, 103–4
people of alms, 99
people of patient forbearance, 98–99
People of the Book, 27, 29, 30–31,
    32, 56, 78, 81, 119–20, 134–
    35, 168–69
people of trials, 100
Persian Gulf states, 114–15
Pharaoh, 106, 159–60
poll tax, 29–31, 71, 78
*The Preparation of the Patiently
    Forbearing Ones and Treasures
    of the Grateful Ones*, 108, 122
Prince Waleed bin Talal Center
    for Muslim-Christian
    Understanding, 180
Protected People, 127
pundits, 100–1, 171–72

Qabil and Habil, 157
Qadri, Muhammad Tahir-ul,
    144, 147
al-Qaeda, 93, 175–77
al-Qaradawi, Yusuf, 129
Qatada ibn Diama, 26–27, 28
Qaynuqa, 87, 140–41
qital, 12, 17–18, 66, 83–84, 100, 102,
    138, 160–61
Qom, 122–23
Quran
    2:62, 32
    2:108, 149
    2:109, 119–20, 134
    2:143, 130
    2:154, 41–42
    2:190, 19–20, 45, 71, 74,
        80, 81, 83

2:191, 81–82
2:192, 19–20
2:193, 34–35, 36, 81–82
2:194, 45–46
2:195, 44, 91–92, 127
2:208, 140–41
2:216, 37–39, 81, 119–20
2:237, 97
2:256, 23, 25–26, 36–37, 56,
    135, 159
2:258, 44
3:98, 41–42
3:104, 11–12
3:110, 11–12
3:169, 41–42
3:200, 13, 96, 97–98, 107, 109–10
4:29, 44, 127, 143
4:74, 41–42
4:75, 22
4:75-76, 136–37
4:90, 25–29, 33
4:93, 44–45, 127
4:94, 40–41
4:95, 17–18
4:100, 43
5:2, 45
5:8, 45
5:27-31, 157, 158
5:32, 44–45
5:33-34, 45, 92
5:48, 34
5:51, 168–69
5:69, 32
5:82, 134–35
6:19, 41–42
6:108, 34
6:151, 44–45
7:137, 106
7:159, 32
7:199, 97
8:39, 34–36
8:61, 24, 25, 26–27, 33, 83–84,
    135, 142–43, 148–49
8:72, 22

Quran (*cont.*)
  9:5, 26–29, 78–79, 81–82, 83–84,
    119–20, 134–35, 136–37, 140
  9:6, 140
  9:12-13, 21–22, 135
  9:23, 33–34
  9:29, 29, 30, 31–32
  9:41, 11, 81–82
  9:71, 11–12
  9:106, 34
  9:111, 25, 41–42
  9:112, 11–12
  9:115, 31
  9:122, 81–82
  10:25, 149, 160–61
  10:56, 44
  10:99, 23, 25–26
  11:118-119, 136
  15:94, 81
  16:110, 15, 95
  16:125, 34, 81
  17:23-24, 33–34
  17:33, 127
  18:29, 56
  21:107, 141–42
  22:17, 34
  22:39-40, 17–18, 19–20, 81
  22:41, 11–12
  22:58, 42–44, 61
  22:78, 13–15, 156
  25:52, 13–14, 102, 139, 156
  25:63, 148–49
  25:72, 97
  25:75, 13, 54
  28:54, 106
  29:8, 33–34
  29:46, 34
  29:69, 13–14
  31:14-15, 33–34
  39:10, 13, 98–99, 106
  41:34, 34
  41:53, 41–42
  42:39, 156
  42:40, 45–46

  42:40-43, 16
  47:4, 25, 26–27, 77, 78–79
  47:31, 17, 95
  48:25, 127
  58:22, 33–34
  59:9, 97
  60:7-8, 28
  60:7-9, 23, 25
  60:8, 24, 33, 56
  60:8-9, 83–84
  109:6, 56
Quraysh, 21, 51, 155
al-Qurtubi, 21, 24, 30–31, 39, 43
Qutb, Muhammad, 125
Qutb, Sayyid, 115–19, 123–24, 125

rabitu, 109–10
Ramadan, 10, 52–53
Rambo III, 170–71
al-Razi, Fakhr al-Din, 14, 19, 20,
    21, 24, 27, 28, 38–39, 80, 83,
    96, 97–98
Realpolitik, 4–5, 74, 88–89, 94
*Reel Bad Arabs: How Hollywood
    Vilifies a People*, 174
Rehab, Ahmed, 163
The Reliance of the Traveler, 83
Republican Turks, 111–12
*The Revival of the Religious
    Sciences*, 106
ribat, 109–10, See also *murabata*
Rida, Rashid, 91, 168
Riyadh, 113–14
Roof, Dylan, 173
Rules of Engagement, 174–75
Russell Berrie
    Foundation, 178–79
Russia, 176

Sabeans, 32
sabr, 5, 6, 7, 12–13, 66, 94–96, 97,
    98–99, 100, 101–4, 106, 107,
    108–9, 151, 152, 155–56
al-sabirun, 96, 98–99

Sadat, Anwar, 119
Sageman, Marc, 177–78
Sahih, 48, 52, 53–54, 76
Said, Jawdat, 151–52, 156–57, 159
Said Nursi, 151–52
Salafi circles, 108
salam, 149
Salam Institute, 152
al-Sarakhsi, 73–74, 78–79, 82
Satha-Anand, Chaiwat, 152
Saudi Arabia, 9, 113–14
School of Salamanca, 165
scriptuaries, 29–30
Seljuq period, 87–88
September 11, 3, 112–13, 125–
    26, 163–64
    attacks, 124–25, 129, 142, 160–
    61, 171–72
al-Shafii, 72, 73, 77, 78, 80–83, 87–
    88, 89–90
Shafii school of law, 72, 77, 81, 145
Shah of Iran, 123
shahada, 41–42
Shaheen, Jack, 174–75
shahid, 41–42, 57
Shaltut, Mahmud, 91, 168
Sharia, 43, 88–89, 138, 149
    "creeping," 178
al-Shaybani, Muhammad, 165–66
Shia, 49, 64–65
Signposts along the Way, 117
al-silm, 140–41
siyar, 84–85, 88–89, 165, 167–68
Southern Poverty Law Center,
    179, 181–82
Soviet Union, 125
Spanish Reconquista, 39
Spencer, Robert, 177–78
spiritual struggle, 6, 65–66, 100,
    103, 107, 109, 123–24, 162
Stop Islamization of
    America, 177–78
Suarez, Francisco, 165
Successor, 26–27, 41

al-Suddi, 27
Sufi
    practices, 113–14
    scholars, 66–67
Sufism, 103, 105. *See also*
    mysticism
Sufyan al-Thawri, 80
suicide, 4, 44, 65, 91, 127–29
    attack(s), 91, 126,
    127–29, 143 (*see also*
    martyrdom operations)
    bombing(s), 4, 6, 126–28,
    143, 144, 160–61 (*see also*
    martyrdom operations)
    terrorism, 144
sunna, 4–5, 27, 47, 70–71, 86, 88,
    90–91, 142
sword verse, 26, 28–29, 134. *See
    also* ayat al-sayf
Syria, 93, 113–14, 129–30, 156–57

al-Tabari, Muhammad ibn Jarir,
    13, 20–21, 26–28, 30–31, 35–
    36, 40, 42–43, 98–99, 134
takfir, 115
al-Takruri, Nawwaf, 128–29
Taliban, 171
terrorism, 4, 44–45, 46, 92, 93, 125–
    26, 130–31, 144, 145, 146–47,
    171–72, 173–74, 176–77
terrorist(s), 46, 65, 126, 171–72,
    173–74, 177–78
al-Tirmidhi, 63, 66–67
Transformative Peace, 152
Treaty of al-Hudaybiyya, 155
Trump, Donald, 3, 179
Trump presidency, 179
Tsarnaev, Tamerlan and
    Dzhokar, 173
Turkey, 79, 122–23, 151–52
Turks, 82, 111–12
Tus, 105
Twelver Shia, 123
Twelvers, 64–65

Umar ibn al-Khattab, 29–30, 71–72
Umayyad
  armies, 62–63
  caliphate, 90–91
  period, 20, 30, 82–83, 87–88
  rulers, 62–63, 79
Umm Umara, 85–86
umma, 139–40
wasat, 130
umra, 19–20, 50
United Nations, 169–70
  Charter, 166–67
United States, 7, 92, 115–16, 117,
    122–23, 125–26, 130–31,
    152, 171–73, 174–75, 178–
    79, 180–82
United States Institute of
  Peace, 152
University of Jeddah, 125
Urwa ibn al-Zubayr, 35, 36–37
US Capitol, 172
US Marines, 174–75
al-Uthayman, Muhammad ibn
  Salih, 143
Uthman ibn Affan, 30
Utmanzai, 153
Utoya Island, 176–77

vali-ye faqih, 122–23
Vichy France, 118–19

Wahhabi
  circles, 108
  ideology, 115
  missionaries, 114
  principles, 114
  proselytization, 114–15
Wahhabis, 114–15
Wahhabism, 113–14
al-Wahidi, Ahmad, 21, 28, 38
wali, 33
Wall Street Journal, 178–79
Washington, D.C., 152
Washington Post, 176–77
Washington Times, 178–79
Western colonialism, 111–12
Western Europe, 7
*While Europe Slept: How Radical
    Islam is Destroying the West
    from Within*, 177
Wilders, Geert, 177
Wisconsin, 173

Yasin, Zayed, 162
Yemen, 174–75
YouTube, 183

Zakat, 26
al-Zamakhshari, 15, 27, 110
Zoroastrians, 29–30, 78
al-Zuhayli, Wahba, 166–67